Joyce Ann Brown: Justice Denied

Melissa Kim

JOYCE ANN BROWN: JUSTICE DENIED

Joyce Ann Brown
with Jay Gaines

THE NOBLE PRESS, INC.

CHICAGO

Printed in the United States of America

Library of Congress Cataloging-in-Publication Data

Brown, Joyce Ann.

    Joyce Ann Brown : justice denied.

      p. cm.

    ISBN 0-9622683-5-6 : $11.95

    1. Brown, Joyce Ann. 2. Women prisioners—Texas—Biography.

I. Title.

HV9468.B755A3   1990

364.1'523'092—dc20

[B]   90-61626

                              CIP

The names of some of the individuals, as well as some of the circumstances, in this book have been changed to protect people's privacy.

Cover photograph by Thomas Lascher
Cover design by Lyn Pusztai and Lee Anne Unterbrink

Noble Press books are available in bulk at discount prices. Single copies are available prepaid direct from the publisher.

Marketing Director
The Noble Press, Inc.
213 W. Institute Place, Suite 508
Chicago, Illinois 60611

With thanks to the Lord, who never left me, forsook me or deceived me, and by whose Grace so many came into my life to help free me from bondage.

Contents

Foreword

Into your life someone occasionally enters who makes such an impact that you can never be the same. Such a person can touch your heart, can alter your very personality and thought.

It may not necessarily be a dynamic and charismatic personality who fires your soul with excitement; sometimes it is a quiet individual, someone whose strength and determination grow on you slowly. Such a person can inspire your spirit to such a degree that the difficult becomes easy, the unthinkable becomes conceivable, and the insurmountable becomes conquerable. Such a person is Joyce Ann Brown.

My first contact with this extraordinary woman resulted from an early 1989 conversation with Jim McCloskey, Director of Centurion Ministries in Princeton, New Jersey. I was interviewing Jim for a magazine article about his ministry, which involves working to free people in prison who have been convicted and sentenced for crimes they did not commit. During our conversation, as Jim was discussing various miscarriages of justice he had uncovered across the country, he mentioned a black woman serving a life sentence in a Texas Department of Corrections prison. Jim exclaimed, "If ever there was a person who should not be in prison, it's Joyce Ann Brown. She did not commit any crime."

I was skeptical, primarily because I tend to assume that whenever people are convicted of a crime, it is because they are guilty. After all, that's what our courts are for—to convict the guilty. Like many people, I never questioned the validity or accuracy of their convictions. I was, of course, familiar with the standard plea "I'm innocent" from those in prison and, like most people, I would nod my head and think to myself, "Sure, that's why you were found guilty!" But that was before I met Joyce.

At Jim's urging, and with the notion of perhaps developing another magazine feature, I decided to look into her case. After several weeks of research, doubts began to nag at my brain. There were too many disturbing coincidences, too many unanswered questions. Even her court-appointed attorney, Kerry Fitzgerald, vehemently proclaimed her innocence and was still battling on her behalf after eight years without pay. I decided to write Joyce, introduce myself, and request her version of the events in the hope of possibly selling it to some magazine. Within a few days she replied.

From the moment I began to read Joyce's account of what she was going through I was "moved to tears, to anger, to frustration," as I later told her, at how she had been railroaded into prison. Yet I was heartened by the warmth and wisdom of her narration. I became a Joyce Ann Brown supporter, and began seeking out ways to get her story heard by those with the power to free her.

I also became a pen pal of Joyce's. We exchanged letters almost daily about her experiences. Before long, I realized that this was not a magazine article but a book waiting to be written. When I first wrote her with this idea, she must have laughed out loud. She wrote back saying I was crazy to think anyone would be interested in what some black woman had to say about her life in prison. But I persisted, and in May of 1989 she sent me the first chapter of what was to become this book.

Each night after work, Joyce would return to her cell and write in long hand on yellow sheets of legal paper, recalling her experiences, pouring out her heart. Slowly the book began to take shape. Upon receiving each segment, I would write back, making suggestions or offering advice. Patiently, she did everything I asked.

Almost everything.

Occasionally, I would read a passage and write back, "Perhaps we need to gloss over this little fact. It makes you look bad." I remember suggesting we more or less skip over her life as a prostitute.

She wrote back, "Jay, what was, was; and there's no changing the facts. If that makes me look bad then it will have to make me look bad, because I can't do anything except tell it the way it happened."

And that's what this book is about: the way it happened. These are the words of an individual who fought for more than nine years in a struggle to prove her innocence and to live with her imprisonment. But it is more than just an account of someone who spent time in prison for a crime she did not commit. It is a lesson in how the human spirit can triumph despite adversity. It is an affirmation of the faith that moves mountains, a testament to the love that changes lives. It is Joyce Ann Brown's story.

Jay Gaines
Richardson, Texas
May 20, 1990

Acknowledgments

There are so many to thank for all that has been done in my behalf. To each and every one I say, "Thank God for you."

And I especially thank the following:

Koquice, my lovely daughter. Even as a child she stood strong and never stopped loving her mom. She handled the situation as an adult from start to finish, and I love her dearly.

Lee Jr., my step-son, who will always be with me in heart and mind.

Brittany Emia LaJoyce, my granddaughter. Grand "T" wasn't there for the beginning, but I'm with her now. And because of this book, there won't be any skeletons.

My precious mom, Ruby. Because of me, she walks with a limp brought on by endless hours of cooking and baking to raise money in my behalf. There are no words to express how deeply my love for her goes.

My daddy, Sylvester Spencer, and my step-daddy, Robert Joe Kelley.

My lovely and strong sisters and brothers: Robert, Horace, Mary, John, Vickie, Jean, Judy, Marvin, and Tangila. They never stopped believing, supporting or loving me.

Kerry Fitzgerald. I know my case became a pain, but not once did he speak of deserting me. Each time there was a legal setback, he worked even harder to get me freed.

Jack Strickland, who came into my life much later and worked with Kerry though he didn't even know me.

Jim McCloskey, Kate Hill, and Richard Reyna. Without these God-sent people, things could not have fallen into place.

Steve McGonigle and Steve Blow of *The Dallas Morning News*, who were the first to tell my story.

Morley Safer of *60 Minutes* and Allen Weissman of *CNN News*. They brought my story out into the open across the country.

My former fellow inmates who helped and supported me throughout the long ordeal: Joyce Ann Logan, my "Sis," without whose assistance and encouragement I might not have undertaken this book; Carla Hogue, who provided me with support and her penmanship; and wonderful Margaret Thomas who took care of me.

Dallas County Commissioner John Wiley Price and Betty Culbreath, chairperson of the Dallas planning commission, for providing me the opportunity to become employed again.

Mary-Terese Cozzola, who so patiently and lovingly helped me with this manuscript.

And last but not least, the man behind the scenes, my blessing, Jay Gaines.

1

A Better Life

We had one of those old type washers, with the wringer mounted on the side. I would push the clothes through the rollers and Joyce would turn the handle, wringing the water out. On that particular day, we were washing diapers. Seems like we were always washing diapers, because as soon as MaDear had one baby, she'd be pregnant with another. So there were always diapers and clothes to wash.

Neither one of us had a warm coat, but we would run outside into the freezing cold to hang those diapers up to dry. Before we could even get the clothespin on, however, the diaper would freeze into a hard white board. Then Joyce and I would run back into the house, warm our hands over the heater, grab a few more diapers, run outside, and hang up some more to freeze in the wind.

On one of our return trips, Joyce looked at me and said, "When I'm grown up my kids will never have to go through what I'm going through. I'm going to make a better life for them." She looked around at the little ones playing on the old linoleum floor—Tangila, Marvin, Vickie, Judy, and Jean—and she added, "I'm going to make a better life for them too."

Joyce kept her promise. After she left home and went out on her own, none of us kids ever had to do without anything.

–Mary Black
Joyce Ann's sister

October 8, 1980. It was a day that I will never forget: It was the day I became caught up in a nightmare that was to stretch into more than nine years.

I had been in court for a total of eight days. Each day I would arrive, take my seat at the table, and wait for the judge and jurors to enter the courtroom. Normally, of course, there would be twelve sitting in the jury box, but on the sixth day of my trial one of the jurors was out sick and my attorney suggested that it might be best to continue with eleven rather than face any postponements or delays. I agreed, but it may have been the worst choice I've ever made in my life. A twelfth juror might have made a difference.

On that day in October, sitting close to the jurors, I was not concerned that my fate rested in the hands of eleven white men and women. I had faith in the system. If you did a crime, you did the time. If you were innocent, you went free. I hadn't done anything—certainly not the terrible thing that the district attorney kept saying I had done—so there was no way the jury could find me guilty. Justice would prevail.

Throughout the trial, my attention was divided between the legal proceedings and my family. I couldn't help worrying about about how my two young children were handling what was happening. They needed reassurance that all the nasty stuff being said about me in the courtroom, on television, and in the newspapers was a lie. It was important to hold them and talk to them to erase the terrible picture of me that the district attorney was creating; but from my seat at the defendant's table, I was helpless.

Finally, each side rested its case and the jury was sent behind closed doors to deliberate. I kept telling myself that in thirty minutes, maybe an hour, I would be able to get my life back to normal. I began to figure out how to explain to the children why our lives had been so terribly disrupted. Perhaps we would take a little trip together, just the three of us, before I set out to find a new job. I knew one thing: my first priority was to help them forget this traumatic episode and return our lives to normalcy as quickly as possible.

As I looked behind me, I could see the family sitting just a few rows back—my children, my mama, all my brothers and sisters, aunts and uncles, and even my ex-husband's mother. I felt the tears building up in my eyes as I looked into each face, remembering all the good times in our lives, lives that had always known only love for each other.

Growing up, we didn't know we were poor. Our family of ten lived in a three-bedroom rented house in Dallas, just off the Central Expressway, in one of several (segregated pockets of poverty) which the city of Dallas tried to keep hidden from the rest of the world. It was not a big city ghetto, but I can assure you our neighborhood was not on the Chamber of Commerce's guided tour program. The houses were run-down and even, in many cases, falling down. They barely provided sufficient protection from the elements; but it was home to us.

Home was all six of us girls sleeping in one room, the four boys in another, and our parents, MaDear and MyDaddy, in the third. I didn't learn why we called our parents "MaDear" and "MyDaddy" until years after I had left home. It was my mama's idea. When we were young, we called the grandparents on our father's side "Big Daddy" and "Big Mama." The grandparents on our mother's side were called "Mama" and "Daddy." To eliminate confusion, we were taught to call our parents "My Mama" and "My Daddy." No one thought it strange when we addressed our father with a question like, "MyDaddy, can we go outside and play?" Along the way, "My Mama" became MaDear because one of the kids couldn't say Mama.

All the kids slept on roll-away beds which could be folded up and pushed to the side during the day. At night, we girls would talk and giggle and carry on until MaDear lost her patience and came into the room to whomp the nearest on the head.

We played all sorts of games at night. Usually make-believe games. Or sometimes we would sit in the dark, very still and quiet, with a shoe in our hand. Then one of the girls would jump out of bed, turn the light on, and we would all lean over the edge of the bed and begin pounding on the floor, killing the cockroaches which had ventured out from behind the walls. Whoever killed the most roaches won the game. We always killed a lot of roaches.

Our days were regimented. MaDear would wake us up for school. We would drag ourselves out of bed, get dressed, and before we could leave the room we had to clean it and make sure it was spotless. For breakfast we would eat whatever was left over from the night before. It was my job to make bologna sandwiches for everyone's school lunch.

After school, we would do our chores. Then we'd either play with the younger kids or help in the kitchen. Most times we worked with babies anchored on our hips. To balance, you had to sort of stand at an angle with your hip sticking out. My sister Mary used to say, "We going to grow up crooked from carrying these kids on our hips."

We never went to bed hungry. Every night we had either potatoes or red beans and hot water corn bread. And we always had chicken. MaDear could do more with a chicken than any woman I've ever known. She could cut a chicken into more parts than any butcher would dream possible. I remember once, Mary and I had to go to one of those big supermarkets, and as we examined the meat case, she let out a squeal of amazement. I looked over and saw her examining a package of cut-up chicken. She thought the butcher was cheating people because there were only half as many pieces in the package as MaDear would have had.

"When I get big, I'll never eat chicken again, as long as I live," Mary used to say. I couldn't blame her. It was the only meat we ever had. None of us kids liked chicken, but we ate it and we always fought to see who would get the piece with the wishbone. After we let it dry out on the window ledge above the sink, whoever had eaten that piece got to make a wish before pulling it. When it was my turn, I always wished for a wonderful dream to come true. I wished big.

As I look back, I think MaDear spent more time on clothing all us kids than on any other chore. The only time we got new clothes was for the first day of school. That was like a holiday because we could expect a brand new pair of shoes or a new dress. The rest of the year, garage sales were our shopping centers. MaDear spent Saturdays going from one to another and combing the Salvation Army Retail Store. She would leave early in the morning and wouldn't get home until late in the afternoon, but she always returned with clothes for the family. They were good clothes even though they were second- or third-hand. MaDear had a knack for searching out the best for the least amount of money.

Sometimes, though, she goofed.

One afternoon she came home with a coat for Mary that, according to Mary, was the ugliest coat ever made. It was orange and black with wide stripes and big padded shoulders.

"MaDear, I ain't wearing that thing."

"You be wearing it, girl. You got no choice. It's the only coat I'm going to buy you. It's warm and it's heavy."

Lord, how Mary hated that coat. She'd put it on without saying a word and leave the house for school. But a block later she would shuck it into a bag and walk, freezing, the rest of the way.

We didn't have a lot of toys to play with, but what we had we enjoyed to the fullest. A jump rope was a favorite, as were dolls, of course. But often we had dolls without any hair, and we hated those. Sometimes we would make our own. We'd take a milk bottle, paint a face on it, stuff a rope in the bottleneck for hair, and that was our "baby."

As black kids in a poor black housing development, it would have been easy to fall prey to drugs, robbery, and other temptations that presented themselves. But all of us stayed away from drugs and gangs and violence and saved MaDear that heartache. We did mess up every now and then like kids do, but Mama would straighten us out on the spot. We lived in fear of her wrath.

One time Mama sent Mary to the corner store to get something she needed for dinner. While Mary was in the store, she picked up a candy bar and put it in her pocket. Poor Mary. The clerk at the cash register saw her, and when she stepped up to the checkout counter to pay for the item Mama wanted, he turned to his brother and said, "I think we have a little thief here. She stole a candy bar."

The other man thought for a moment and said, "I guess we had better call the police."

Mary's eyes got as big as saucers, but they got even bigger when the clerk said, "No, we don't need to call the police. We'll just call her mama."

Mary started crying. "No, don't call my mama!" she sobbed. "Call the police." She knew what would happen if MaDear found out what she had done.

Sure enough. MaDear came bouncing into that store and grabbed Mary by the ear. First she made her apologize and then, right there, in front of God and everyone, she whipped Mary for stealing. I guess today they would call such a spanking "child abuse," but I'll tell you one thing—Mary never stole again.

By 1965 dramatic changes were taking place in Dallas. Integration reached us. Although it was hailed by our nation's leaders as great progress, back in our neck of the city it only made us realize how poor we were. In an all black school, it didn't matter how much you had, because none of the other kids had anything either. With integration, however, poor black kids were thrown in with white kids who seemed to have everything.

By the time schools were integrated I had graduated from high school and was working nights on the assembly line at a large computer manufacturer. My brothers and sisters, Vickie, Jean, Judy, Tangila, Mary, and Marvin, were still in school and, like all kids, wanted to participate in the variety of activities available at their new school. Because our parents simply could not afford the extra expense involved, these opportunities threatened to pass them by. I couldn't stand that thought. So I promised them that as long as they stayed in school, they'd never have to miss out on a football game, sock hop, or other special activity.

I kept that promise, but it was rough. Sometimes the money from my job wouldn't last from one payday to the next. The more activities the kids got involved in, the more strapped for money I became.

In 1969 I met James Brown, a drummer in a Dallas dance band. Within a few months we were married, but I guess that was a mistake because our marriage lasted less than a year. James and I separated, but out of that marriage came the most wonderful thing in my life—my daughter Koquice. I can't begin to express the joy and fulfillment I felt when I held her in my arms.

After I separated from James, I took a job at a boat manufacturing company, and it was then that I began to notice something peculiar. White men liked to flirt with me. It could have been because of my figure, my friendly attitude, or who knows why? But even when I was not at work, just walking around a mall or supermarket, I could feel the eyes of white men on me.

One night in a club, a white man approached my table and asked to sit down. He was a gentleman and we spent several hours talking. I felt very comfortable with him and he with me. We even discussed his marital problems. At some point he asked, "Joyce, how do you feel about black and white relationships?"

The idea had previously entered my mind. Even as teenagers, we girls had often wondered what it would be like to date a white boy. We would lie in our beds at night, quietly discussing the idea, but we would always dismiss the subject before we fell asleep. We knew MaDear would beat us within an inch of our lives if she ever caught us with a white boy.

So I answered, "I don't know. I've never been out with a white man."

We talked into the early hours of the morning, and before I finally left for the night we made a date for another evening. As I left, he put something in my hand. It was money. I was several dollars richer and all I had done was spend some time talking with a white man.

We had another date, then another, and before you know it, one thing led to another and we began sleeping together occasionally. Keep in mind that I was living back at home, so every time the phone rang I would break my neck racing to answer it before anyone else. I especially didn't want MaDear to pick up the phone because she might recognize the voice of a white man, and then I would be in deep trouble.

As our relationship developed, my friend would often ask how things were going. When I would tell him what I was doing for my family, like buying a new dress for Jean or gym shoes for Marvin, he would always hand me the money I needed. Given the size of my paycheck, I needed all the help I could get. In fact, our relationship reached the point where he would just hand me money every week, without my even asking.

Although I came to depend on that "allowance" for keeping my promise to the kids, my friend and I didn't commit ourselves to a long-term relationship. I continued to date other men, including other white men. Many of them would press a few bills into my hand when they dropped me off at home. Believe it or not, not all of them were after sex—some just wanted to dance or talk or see a movie. There were those who wanted sex, of course, but I slept with them if I cared for them, and if I wanted to. I didn't go to bed with them because of the money, but I didn't object to receiving it either.

At that time, I had no idea I was engaging in prostitution. Anyone suggesting such a thing would have been in for a fight. I simply looked upon the men as people I was dating who wanted no strings attached. It was a good situation for me because I didn't want any strings either.

In 1970, I took a job in a high school community guidance center. Not only did I make better money there, but I also met other white men who wanted to date me. I continued to help out my brothers and sisters, and even started saving for Koquice and me to move into a place of our own.

I had a girlfriend who was actually involved in prostitution, but I would get so angry whenever anyone called her a whore. "Men just like to give her money," I would say in her defense. One day when I was home alone, one of my dates came over. Before we said goodbye, he put some money on my dresser. My girlfriend showed up just after he left and the first thing she noticed was that money sitting on the dresser.

"What's that for?" she asked.

"My friend left it to help me out," I answered.

"Do you know what you're doing, girl?"

"What do you mean, what am I doing?"

"You're doing the same thing I do."

I looked at her in disbelief. "You're lying. I'm not a prostitute. He's just a friend of mine helping me out."

"Oh, yeah. Those men I date who leave money on my dresser are also friends of mine."

I said, "Oh girl, you go out looking for men. I don't look for them. They call me. They're friends that come by to visit with me."

She just shook her head and we didn't talk about it anymore.

Then one night I met this white man at a lounge. We danced and talked and just had a great time. He drank a great deal of liquor while I had soft drinks because I don't drink, and when he asked me to go back to his hotel room with him, I agreed.

When we entered his room, he shocked me by asking, "Are you a hooker?"

Offended, I literally screamed out, "Of course not!"

"Then what are you doing in my room?"

"Because you're nice and friendly," I snapped. "That's the only reason I came to your room with you."

"That's exactly the way hookers work, Joyce." He sat me down and explained that vice officers often pick up girls in a lounge, ask them to come to their room, and when they do, immediately arrest them. As he put it, if he had been a policeman I would have been busted for prostitution. "But," he went on, "if you do go back to a man's room, get your money first. Because after you make love, you can't make a man pay. You can't whip him and you can't make a scene because you'll get arrested. You need to get your money first." That got me to thinking. The extra money certainly came in handy for my daughter, as well as for the rest of the family. If I was going to do it, I might as well do it right. I decided to start dating lots of white men and make lots of money.

In the months that followed, I made more in one night than I could in several weeks of my day job. And I needed it. Koquice was growing quickly and I wanted her to have the best of everything. My brothers and sisters had the opportunity to get college educations and better jobs, but to get them they needed help with tuition, nice clothes, and other necessities.

Robert, the oldest, was our pride and joy. He was a Peace Corps volunteer serving in Morocco and was the first of our family to graduate from college. Not only did he earn his Bachelor's degree but his Master's as well. I was so proud of him I could pop. During his visits home from college, I loved being able to surprise him with a new sweater, a pair of shoes, or just some spending money.

For me, Robert was the symbol of what my brothers and sisters could become if they stayed in school. As far as I was concerned, they *would* stay in school by any means necessary. If that meant being a full-time prostitute, so be it. All I could see was the amount of money I was making and how much it was helping the family.

I also helped out in other ways. MaDear was so strict that the younger ones would get me to run interference whenever they wanted to do something other than schoolwork or chores. For example, I might go over to the house and say, "Jean and Vickie want to go to the ball game, so I'm going to take them."

"I ain't got no extra money for such foolishness," MaDear would say.

"Don't worry about it, Mama, I'll take care of everything." And away we would go. I would drop them off, give them pocket money, and come back later to pick them up.

Around that time, black football teams like Grambling and Prairieview were becoming popular with Dallas teenagers who would drive anywhere in the state to watch them play. I would loan the kids my car and off they would go, as far as Houston sometimes, to see their black heroes. While they were gone, I would leave my phone off the hook so MaDear couldn't call and ask for them. When they returned, I would take them home as if they had been with me the whole time. We thought we were pretty clever, but MaDear knew what we were up to.

Late in 1971 I began dating Lee Visor. Lee was a lot of fun to be with, although his profession wasn't exactly above reproach. Lee was a hustler and would make a dollar any way he could. He had a beautiful little boy, Lee Jr., who was just a few months older than Koquice, and the two got along like brother and sister. Soon we decided we all needed to be together. I was not ready to get married again, so we lived together as a family and I raised Lee Jr. like he was my own flesh and blood.

My relationship with Lee Sr. was less traditional. He made no proprietary demands on me and I made none on him; consequently we got along very well. When we first set up house together I told Lee I intended to stay in prostitution for another few years, save as much money as possible, and then get out. That was fine with him. I did my thing, he did his. We moved into a nice home in Garland where we rented with an option to buy. I fixed the place up real nice and it was a good home. Like the home I was raised in, it was a happy home.

As the years slipped by, I continued using and relying on the money I made from prostitution. After six years I was still essentially a call girl, though Lee and I managed to keep it a secret from the family. My only brush with exposure was a single arrest for aggravated promotion of prostitution. A mug shot was taken of me, but the charge was dropped before anyone could find out. It was like living a double life. I made sure I was in church most Sundays and dressed very conservatively around the family. MaDear certainly didn't know what I was up to. My brothers and sisters may have suspected something, but maybe they just didn't want to find out for sure. I certainly did everything I could to keep them from finding out. I even had a "front" job, a place of where I worked part-time to maintain an image of respectability.

One spring afternoon in 1979, Koquice and Lee Jr. came in as I was preparing for work and asked, "Mama, can we go with you?" At the time, I was working as a hostess at a family restaurant. I thought it might be nice to have them visit, so they got dressed and came along. That was the day I decided to get out of the business.

My babies were sitting in a booth, enjoying themselves while the waitresses and regular customers made a big play over them. I was watching from my station near the entrance when a man walked up and whispered in my ear, "Hello, Joyce. Come see me when you get off."

Quickly, I looked over at Lee and Koquice to make sure they had not heard him. In that moment, a feeling of guilt and shame flooded over me. What would they think if they knew what their mama really did for a living?

It hit me. "This isn't for me."

That night I explained to Lee what had happened and told him I was "retiring" from the business. It didn't matter to him. As long as my plans didn't interfere with his lifestyle, he didn't care what I did. Besides, our relationship was falling apart by then. Although he still lived in my home, he was gone most of the time and we didn't see him for weeks on end.

The following day, I went out looking for a real job. I even got my family and friends to ask around for me. Then a friend called. "Joyce, I heard of a good job for you and I know you can do it."

I took down the information, applied for the job, and soon began working full-time as a "Girl Friday" at Koslow's Furs. I typed, answered the phone, kept the books, paid bills. . .all the miscellaneous duties that crop up in any office.

Sometimes I would just look at my paycheck and laugh. What I made in a week at Koslow's, I could have made in an hour as a prostitute. But it was a good, clean check. I was working hard and was proud of my work. And I could go home and spend the entire evening with Lee Jr. and Koquice.

One Saturday it snowed and I called my boss, Mr. Dupler, to ask if I could bring them to work with me because the roads were too bad to make it to the baby sitter's. He assured me that was fine, and so we all bundled up, got in the car, and took the long, slippery journey to Koslow's.

When we got there, Mr. Dupler put Koquice and Lee Jr. to work. Koquice became the "waitress" and served coffee to employees and customers. Lee Jr. went to the storage room and helped out back there. At the end of the day, Mr. Dupler paid both of them out of his pocket and bragged about how great they were. Was I a proud mama? What do you think? It was a sight to behold.

On May 6, 1980, sometime around noon, I was answering the telephone at Koslow's when a call came in for Mr. Dupler. I put the caller through and a few minutes later, Mr. Dupler came out and said, "There's been a robbery at another furrier's. The robbers shot the owner and the police want us to be on the alert." We talked about the robbery for a moment and then went back to work.

Three days later, on a Friday morning, I was getting ready for work when the phone rang. It was MaDear.

"Joyce, are you all right?"

"Of course I'm all right," I laughed. "I'm getting ready for work. What do you want?"

She hesitated a moment and then said, "DeeDee just called and said there's a story in the morning paper that the police are looking for you about a fur robbery."

"Say what?"

"DeeDee says the police want to talk to you."

I couldn't believe it. "Well, DeeDee must be reading wrong because the police don't want to talk to me about anything. She's just made a mistake." Then I told her I had to go or I'd be late for work.

Five minutes later, the phone rang again. It was MaDear, and this time her voice really sounded scared.

"Joyce, Miss Nannie just called and she told me the same thing DeeDee did. There's a story in the paper about the police looking for you."

"Mama, just wait a minute. I'll run down and get a morning paper and see what everyone is so upset about. I'll call you back."

Cursing at the time, knowing I'd be late for work, I threw on a coat and ran out to pick up a copy of *The Dallas Morning News*. When I saw the story, my heart stopped. The police were indeed looking for me in connection with the robbery of Fine Furs By Rubin and the murder of its owner, Rubin Danziger. My hands were shaking as I read that the police had been searching for me but believed that I had fled to Denver.

What were they talking about? Fled to Denver? I hadn't even been out of town. Why did they want to talk to me? What could I possibly know that would help their investigation?

I dashed back home and called the police department. I had a few friends who were cops, but I couldn't reach any of them. Finally I talked to a lieutenant I had met, and when I asked him if the police were looking for me, he answered, "I've heard a rumor to that effect, Joyce, but I'm not sure about it."

"Well, I'm coming down there to straighten all this out," I told him.

Then I called Robert Rose, an attorney I knew. When I told him about the story in the paper he said, "Joyce, don't go down there without an attorney. Come to my office and wait here while I check on what's going on."

I knew I hadn't done anything wrong and didn't understand why I needed to go to the police station with a lawyer. Lawyers were for guilty people, not innocent ones. But I did as Robert asked.

When we arrived, I was questioned and then told to wait in a small room where I sat for about three hours, without any idea of what was happening. I learned later that while I was sitting in that room, the police were ransacking my home looking for evidence that would link me to the fur robbery. Needless to say, they didn't find anything.

Eventually, an officer came in and began to question me. Over and over again I told him where I had been all day on May sixth—at work at Koslow's—and over and over again, he kept saying, "You're lying. We know you pulled that robbery."

That made me mad. "A liar I'm not. I told you where I was. I was at work, at Koslow's Furs. You can check there and they'll tell you the same thing."

The officer said, "We know you left work, went and robbed that store, and returned to work. We have an eyewitness who has iden-tified you."

Robert requested a lineup, but the officer said he didn't need one because a witness had already picked my picture out of a photograph lineup. It was then I realized my past had caught up with me. I remembered my arrest from years ago, and the cop's parting com-ment when my charges were dropped: "Now we have your picture on file." With that mug shot, I was identified by the widow of the man shot in the robbery as one of two women who had participated in the robbery and murder.

I was booked on two charges, aggravated robbery and capital murder. At the time, they kept asking me if I knew a David Shafer, and I kept repeating, "I don't know any David Shafer."

"We arrested him near your house because he drove the getaway car."

When I was taken down to be arraigned, someone pointed David Shafer out. I didn't know him, and didn't know why he was there, but I didn't have time to worry about it because suddenly I found myself trapped. I was charged and thrown into a cell. My bail was set at one million dollars. My nightmare had begun.

2

Pulling Chain

On May 9, 1980, I was working on the starter of a friend's car when the police suddenly arrived, jumped out of their car, pointed a gun at me, and told me to raise my hands. One policeman said, "I've got one question: Where are the furs?"

I didn't know what he was talking about. They questioned me a bit longer and then arrested me, put me in the squad car, and headed for jail. On the way, one of the officers said, "You must be a nigger lover."

They booked me for aggravated robbery and capital murder, even though I kept telling them over and over that I didn't know what they were talking about. I even told them that at the time they said I robbed a fur store, I was having lunch with my fiancee and her boss, a dentist.

They kept telling me that the lady who had been robbed had identified my picture as the red-haired, red-bearded man who drove the getaway car. I kept telling them it was a mistake.

The following day, twenty-four hours after being arrested, they found out I was telling the truth and that Mrs. Danziger had made a mistake in identifying me. They let me out of jail with no explanation, no apology, no good-bye.

To add insult to injury, it cost me more than five hundred dollars to get my arrest removed and erased from police files.

—David Shafer
Garland, Texas

A one million dollar bond! Even when they moved me to the county jail and my bond was reduced to $500,000, I still couldn't believe it. Not only was I being falsely accused, but I was being held where I couldn't do anything to prove my innocence. Meanwhile, Robert explained that he had no experience in handling capital murder cases and could not represent me.

Broke, still in shock, and trapped in a county jail cell, I had little choice but to accept the court's offer of a court-appointed attorney. Kerry P. Fitzgerald was assigned to my case.

Tall, handsome and confident, Kerry made me feel better the moment I met him. He sat down with me and said his first priority was to get my bail lowered. I really didn't think he would be successful in his attempt, but within a few weeks there was a hearing and my bond was lowered to $25,000.

My family tried to make me as comfortable as possible while they struggled to get every cent together for the bond money. They visited as much as they could and ensured that I would not do without anything like toothpaste, shampoo or other commissary items by providing me with the maximum amount of spending money inmates were allowed—$35 a week. This was more than I really needed, but they continued to send it. Since inmates could not let money build up on the books, I used the surplus to help less fortunate inmates buy what they needed.

After fifty-one days, my family had scraped up the bond money and I walked out of county jail. As soon as I posted bail, however, the court informed me that since my family had made bond, I was no longer entitled to a court-appointed attorney and would have to make arrangements to obtain a lawyer at my own expense. Kerry Fitzgerald had impressed me, so I went to see him. He agreed to take on my case, and again my family got behind me and came up with the necessary deposit to retain his services.

But we couldn't raise any more money. Several months went by and I couldn't make the second installment. Another woman had taken my place at Koslow's, and I couldn't get another job. Who would hire a black woman waiting to go on trial for aggravated robbery and capital murder? So Lee Jr. went to stay with his father's mother, who lived in Dallas, and Koquice and I moved back to MaDear's to wait for the trial. I returned to court and requested another court-appointed attorney. The Lord was looking out for me because the court granted the request. Guess who was appointed? Kerry P. Fitzgerald.

My family put the word out on the street through friends and neighbors for anyone with any information concerning the robbery to come forward.

In the meantime, the police learned that one of the women involved in the robbery was a Rene Taylor. According to the papers, the police were looking for her. I kept praying they would find her before my trial began because I knew she could clear my name by admitting I was not her accomplice. But the police search was unsuccessful and no one came forward from the streets. Rene Taylor remained at large.

On September 29, 1980, my trial began. The prosecution set out to prove that on May 6, 1980, at approximately one o'clock in the afternoon, two black women wearing jogging suits and scarves entered Fine Furs By Rubin, robbed the store and shot the owner, Rubin Danziger, in cold blood. According to the district attorney, a woman dressed in blue—who allegedly was me—had come into the furriers the previous week and had asked Mr. and Mrs Danziger about having a fur hat and collar made.

Mrs. Danziger testified that when her husband, a fifty-four-year-old survivor of a Nazi prison camp, went to the rear of the store, the woman in pink followed and shoved him up against the wall. Then she shot him, and while the woman in blue looked on, she shouted at Mrs. Danziger to stuff furs into the black plastic garbage bags they had brought. As Mrs. Danziger did so, the woman in pink kicked her and threatened to shoot her. She fired a shot, but it missed and struck the store's front window instead.

Mrs. Danziger saved her own life by telling the women that she had terminal cancer and had only weeks to live. Upon hearing that, the pink-clad woman said, "We'll just let you suffer." Both women then threw her into a storage room and locked the door. Mrs. Danziger estimated that the two women spent between ten and thirty minutes in the store.

The most damaging part of her testimony came when the district attorney asked, "Is the woman who robbed you in the store when your husband was shot in this courtroom?"

Mrs. Danziger looked straight at me and answered, "It's that woman sitting right there."

God, I could have died! The woman was wrong! She had made a mistake and there was nothing I could do about it.

The prosecution also introduced testimony that an informant had called the police station on May 6 and told them Joyce Ann Brown was involved in the robbery. To make matters worse, the next day police had found a brown Datsun abandoned in South Dallas. When they searched the car, they found evidence of the robbery—scarves, fingerprints, and several paper-wrapped coat hangers. In it they also found a car rental contract bearing the signature of a "Joyce Ann Brown" and showing a Denver address and Colorado driver's license number.

Kerry could feel the tension and fear building up in me, so he reached over, patted my hand and whispered, "It's all right. Our turn will come. This is all a bunch of crap." I began to regain my confidence when Kerry started tearing the prosecution's case apart.

To begin with, Kerry disclosed that the brown Datsun had been rented by another woman named Joyce Ann Brown, a Denver resident who freely admitted to having lent the car to her friend Rene Taylor. Several witnesses testified that on the night the car was rented (at a Denver car rental agency), I was at a wedding rehearsal for Thomas Henderson, the former Dallas Cowboy football star.

Police records indicated that the first alarm for the robbery was received at 1:16 p.m. and that the first patrol unit arrived at 1:23 p.m. Seven witnesses, my co-workers at Koslow's Furs, testified that before, during, and after the reported time of the robbery, I was sitting at my desk in my office. Sandy Beahm, one of my co-workers, testified that at 1:19 p.m., she returned from lunch, clocked in (her timecard verified this fact), and walked to my desk to thank me for getting her her paycheck a day early.

Other co-workers, including Mr. Dupler and the assistant manager, also testified that I was at work during the time of the crime.

Kerry also established that while Rene Taylor's fingerprints had been found on the paper-wrapped coat hangers discovered in the getaway car, my prints had not. He further pointed out that although my home had been searched thoroughly after my arrest, not one shred of evidence was ever found to link me to the crime.

The prosecution countered with the theory that although my co-workers could account for most of my day, there was a thirty-minute gap in which no one could actually swear that they talked to me or saw me. They claimed that half an hour was all I needed to leave my desk, change clothes, drive three miles through heavy noon traffic, enter the fur store, rob it, shoot the owner, leave the store, make the three-mile return trip back through north Dallas, change clothes and sit down at my desk as if nothing had happened.

In addition to this far-fetched thirty-minute theory, the prosecution's case rested on Mrs. Danziger's identification of me in a photograph—an identification made only hours after Mrs. Danziger had learned that her husband had died from the gunshot wound.

Kerry was confident that this highly irregular identification would mean little in the face of all the solid evidence pointing to my innocence. We had proof that another Joyce Ann Brown had rented the getaway car in Denver, we had the witnesses from Koslow's, we had timecards verifying my whereabouts, and we had the physical impossibility of getting from Koslow's to the scene of the robbery within the time frame the district attorney had claimed.

But we neglected to take into consideration the aggressive nature of the district attorney.

As their final witness, they called to the stand a Martha Jean Bruce.

"Who is that?" Kerry asked.

"Just a woman I met in jail," I answered, wondering what she was doing there.

"She's probably going to tell a lie then," Kerry guessed.

How right he was!

Martha Jean Bruce was one of the new inmates I had helped in the county jail when I was trying to make bond. I remembered her clearly because I had felt so sorry for her at the time. She could neither read nor write, and had no family on the outside that cared enough to help her. Even though she was what I would call "black trash," I had helped her.

There was an inmate I befriended in jail named Emma. On the day Emma was transferred to a state prison, I promised to drive her children there to visit her once I got out. Martha Jean Bruce heard me make that offer and said something like, "I wish someone would drive my children down to see me."

I had answered, "Get me on your visitors list and I'll bring them to see you when I come to see Emma."

That charitable offer came back to haunt me.

Under oath, Martha Jean Bruce testified that while we were in jail together, I had confessed to committing the crime. She told the jury I bragged about how I had made practice runs from Koslow's to Fine Furs By Rubin. The clincher came when the district attorney asked her if we were friends, and she said, "Yes, she's even on my visitor's list at prison."

With that bombshell, both sides rested and the jury retired to consider my verdict.

As I waited for the jury to return, I received encouragement from almost everyone. Other lawyers would come into the courtroom and speak to Kerry, saying things like, "You've got this one in the bag," or "I don't know why this case was ever brought to trial." Even the court reporter came over and said, "You've won the case."

Yet, one hour went by. Then two hours. And nothing. The jury had retired about one o'clock, and by five I began to get scared. I couldn't understand what was taking so long. Couldn't they see from the evidence that I was not the lady who had been with that Rene Taylor? I wanted to scream out, "Look! If you don't understand something, please talk to me."

The bailiff, sensing my anxiety and fear, walked over to where I was sitting. Placing her hand on my shoulder she said, "Don't worry, Joyce. The longer they are out the better it is."

That made no sense to me and only confused me more, made me more afraid. All kinds of crazy thoughts began to swim around in my head. I began to wonder if they were looking at me as a black woman. What if they were feeling sorry for Mrs. Danziger, the widow, and simply wanted someone to pay for the crime? What if some of the jurors were friends with the D.A.? I started thinking about the way you see the district attorneys portrayed in the movies and how they get one or two of the jurors to do as they want. What if the D.A. controlled my jurors like that?

Slowly I turned into a nervous wreck. I couldn't sit still. I was fidgety. I kept getting up and walking down the hall, and then I would come back and take my seat. I remember I had a piece of paper in my hands and kept twisting it and twisting it and twisting it. When I get nervous, I lose control of my breathing, so every few minutes I had to take sharp, deep lungfuls of air to catch my breath. Then I would get up and walk some more.

The walking also helped keep me from crying. I was determined not to do that. MaDear was in the courtroom and I knew if I broke down, she would break down too. She is the strongest woman I've ever known, but her love for her children is so powerful that she literally lives their pain. Throughout the trial I had insisted she stay away. But there was no keeping her away that day; so, when I felt the tears welling up, I would get up from my seat and walk to the bathroom, wash my face, put my smile back on, and return to the courtroom.

Six hours went by. Then a note was sent out from the jury room asking that a part of the trial records be read again. My heart missed a beat. What could they be puzzled about? My God, wasn't it plain that I was innocent? What else could they possibly need?

One by one, the jurors filed back into the courtroom and took their seats. Judge Chapman read the requested material to them. It had to do with a part of Mrs. Danziger's testimony. The day the trial started, before the jury was present, there had been an identification hearing so that Mrs. Danziger could identify me in person. Up to that point, she had never seen me—only that photograph. During the hearing, she claimed I had once come into her store to get some clothing items cleaned. The jury was not present at that hearing. Later on in the trial, while I was on the stand, I had remembered her statement from the hearing and volunteered before the jury, "I have never gone into her shop to have anything cleaned." Understandably, they were confused.

And so they were questioning certain testimony concerning the cleaning of clothes—something Mrs. Danziger had said in their presence which was inconsistent with the notes from her appearance outside of their presence. Kerry immediately realized the inconsistency and requested that the judge call Mrs. Danziger back to testify before the jury. His request was denied. He then asked the judge to explain to the jury that there had been testimony outside their presence during the identification hearing.

This request was granted, but the explanation was a stream of legalese that would make sense only to a judge or lawyer. I was looking at the faces of the jurors and could see that they didn't understand. But I saw something else and what I saw sent a cold shiver of fear through my body. They wanted to find me guilty. I could see it in their eyes. I saw hatred for me on their faces. One of "them" had been murdered and one of "us" was accused. A Holocaust survivor had been shot in the head and a black nigger woman was on the stand. At that moment, I knew I had been had.

The jury left the courtroom and everyone went out to get a breath of fresh air, but I stayed glued to my seat. I couldn't move. I was shivering with a fear of what was coming. I knew I had to get MaDear out of the courtroom. But before I could catch the attention of a friend sitting in the gallery, I heard the bailiff say, "Oooh, the jury sounds like they're having a party in there."

I couldn't believe my ears. From behind the closed doors of the jury room, those eleven men and women were laughing and cutting up like they were watching a game show. Was this just a big joke to them?

Five minutes later, they returned to the courtroom. I watched as they filed in. There was a shit-eating half-grin on one of the juror's faces that made me feel like I was being mocked. My first thought was, *those prejudiced bastards!* How could I have possibly thought that a black woman could get a fair trial in Dallas? I looked over at my white attorney and wondered if he was a part of all this. I looked at the white judge. How could I have been so stupid? They were all in it together. Fuck them all!

A silence settled over the courtroom, and the jury was asked if they had reached a verdict. The judge was handed their verdict, studied it a moment, then read the words that have burned in my brain ever since: "We the jury find the defendant, Joyce Brown, guilty as charged for aggravated robbery."

"I'm innocent!" I wanted to scream. "You can't send an innocent person to prison!" The image of a woman tied hand and foot and burned alive at the stake flashed through my mind. I felt just as helpless.

I was so wrapped up in my thoughts and had such a horrible feeling of aloneness that I didn't realize for a few moments that Kerry was talking to me. I didn't see him. I didn't see anyone. I was just staring into space, fuming with rage. But finally I realized he was on his knees pleading with me.

"You can't fire me! I won't let you! Those motherfuckers fucked me! I know I won this case! They fucked me! I won't give up on you until you're free!"

And somehow a screaming reached my ears. It was MaDear. My whole body was numb. It was as if I had fallen into a bottomless pit and there was no way to climb out. I barely remember the handcuffs being locked around my wrists and the two men leading me out of the courtroom. I do remember MaDear standing in the hall, crying. As we walked towards her I asked one of the guards if I could talk to her. He nodded yes and we stopped for a moment. But before I could say anything, the other guard—a fat-bellied redneck of a man—pulled me away and said, "Keep moving!"

I was taken to a small cell, a holding tank, and my handcuffs were removed. Then they pushed me inside and slammed the door shut. I was alone.

The cell was bare except for a toilet, which was encrusted with human waste and surrounded by cigarette butts and soiled wads of toilet paper. The smell was nauseating. As I watched hordes of cockroaches dart across the floor, I couldn't help thinking that at least those loathsome little bugs were free. With tears running down my face, I stood there staring at the filthy walls, trying to think things out.

MaDear would take care of Koquice, and Lee Jr. was still living with his father's mother, so I knew both children would be all right until I could get out. But it would be hard on them. They would have to get used to being raised differently from what they were used to. Koquice would have to get used to being raised Mama's way. She would learn that kids are to be seen, not heard. No backtalk or lip allowed. Values and morals and manners would be instilled with a bop on the head, not a word or a long talk. But while MaDear would exercise her firm brand of discipline, she would also shower her with the love and encouragement that had made me into a strong, confident woman. And Lee Jr.'s grandmother would be equally as loving and firm with him as MaDear would be with Koquice. My children would be fine.

But what would they think of me? Would they wonder if I was guilty? Would they be ashamed of me? Stop loving me? Would they hate me?

Taking me away from my babies. This was what the justice system was all about? How I hated "justice" as I finally sat down on the floor of that holding tank. I hated anything and anybody connected to that word. It seemed like just a way of showing me that I was nothing in the white world's eyes. At the time, I thought only blacks were sent to prison for crimes they didn't commit. Later I would discover that it's not only blacks who are victims of our justice system, but Mexicans and poor whites as well.

I remained in a state of shock for hours. Finally, a jailer came to let me out and sent me to be processed and turned over to the county jail where I would spend the next three months.

On the night of January 9, 1981, I was awakened from a deep sleep. The jail intercom was barking out names of prisoners who would "pull chain," the expression used to describe the transporting of prisoners to state prison.

"Joyce Brown!" the loudspeaker barked.

I grabbed my head and cried, "Lord, no." Surely my appeal was just around the corner. Why would they send me all the way to state prison just to have to send me back here for my new trial?

My first thought was to call MaDear and tell her what was going on, but another inmate, Cat, looked at me with pity and said, "You can't, honey. That's why they pull chain late at night—so no one will know you're leaving."

I couldn't believe they would make me leave without calling my mama. What was the harm in our letting our families know where we were going?

January of 1981 was a cold one in Dallas. Bitter cold. Nevertheless, at two o'clock in the morning we were rounded up like a herd of cattle and processed through the jail. Our wrists were handcuffed; anklecuffs were snapped on our legs. A long chain connecting the anklecuffs was stretched out along the ground. After we were hooked up to the chain, we had to walk together as one, in single file and in unison, or be jerked to the ground.

When we got to the check-out point—the Control Room—they made us take off our panties, bra, and socks, because it was against the rules for female prisoners to leave wearing anything except jail issues—a pair of short-sleeve coveralls and a pair of slippers, or "scuffs." Scuffs are made from a double layer of rough white cotton and the toes are cut out, making it difficult to walk. You can't lift your feet because if you do the scuffs fall off. To walk, you have to shuffle your feet along the floor.

There we were, twenty of us chained together, standing in the cold room and shivering in our coveralls and scuffs. We had to stand there without speaking until the jailer finally yelled, "Head 'em up and move 'em out!"

Then we were herded onto a large white bus. Iron benches were bolted to the floor on either side, and we shuffled along to the back of the bus until one of the guards yelled, "Sit!"

The benches were narrow, hard and cold, and since I was chained to the women on either side of me, I couldn't lean back. I could only sit forward, freezing, my back strained to the breaking point. And the smell in there was revolting. I knew I was getting ready to lose my last meal, but Cat, who was sitting next to me, kept whispering, "Baby, hang tough. You got to be strong. If you throw up, they ain't going to clean it and we'll have to ride with it all the way."

I thought to myself, "What if I have to use the bathroom?"

Cat was reading my thoughts and just smiled. "You just have to hold it, Baby." She made a face at the stench and added, "The mens that ride this bus don't give a damn. They just piss whenever they feel like it and they don't care if it's on the floor. That's what the smell is."

While we waited for the bus to get moving, I tried to take my mind off the nauseating stench by taking inventory of my fellow passengers. Cat was the only one I had gotten to know at all, but I had learned something about most of the other women over the past three months.

There was a girl convicted of killing her female lover's new lover, a man. And Minnie, convicted of stealing jewelry and forging checks. There was Missy, who had been convicted of killing her baby, cutting it up and storing the pieces in the freezer. She was sentenced to twenty-five years. Virginia had received twelve years for stabbing her boyfriend to death. Maria was on her way to serve a fifteen-year sentence for setting her house on fire and burning her boyfriend alive. The others were all going to serve out sentences from two to five years for various crimes of theft. With the exception of three or four of us, everyone on the bus was a repeat offender and had made the trip to Huntsville, Texas more than once.

At last, the bus roared up and we left Dallas. As the lights disappeared behind us, I prayed for the strength that only God could give me. I kept wondering if the Texas Department of Corrections (T.D.C.) would be any better, any cleaner. I prayed the whole trip, "Lord, you have said that I'm your child. Help me to carry this weight on my shoulders. What's my fate? Am I to live among women like this my whole life?"

As I prayed, I cried. I cried the entire trip. I was still sure that I was simply having a horrible nightmare. Any minute someone would shake me and say, "Wake up, Joyce." But nobody did. I opened my eyes and faced iron-barred windows. I was on my way to Goree Prison in a big, ugly white bus.

When I saw a sign reading "Huntsville, 5 Miles," I felt I was passing into another world, another time zone. Some of the women on the bus began to laugh and joke. They were going "home." In fact, for many on the bus, it was better than home. They were going to a place that was warm, where there was a bed, hot showers and three hot meals a day. For these women, prison was a paradise, a far better place than whatever homes they might have had.

We finally arrived at what is known as the "Walls Unit," the first stop for incoming prisoners. While T.D.C. guards stood around, staring at us with undisguised lust, smirking and making snide sexual remarks, inmates fingerprinted us, checked our teeth, and processed our records. When that sideshow was over, they loaded us back onto the big white bus for the ride to the Goree Unit, which was the women's prison at the time.

I had cried so much and for so long on the trip from Dallas that I knew I would be sick if I didn't pull myself together. Chained once again in the bus, I made some promises to myself. I vowed not to let the state make an animal out of me. I had seen the effect prison could have on women and it was frightening. In mind, body and spirit, those women had deteriorated beyond recovery. The state could take my freedom, but that was all they were going to get from me. I also swore that I would not cry anymore.

We arrived at Goree around eleven o'clock in the morning, just in time for lunch. While awaiting transfer in the county jail, I had often heard others talk about how much better the food would be in prison. Well, my first meal at T.D.C. was pure slop, some kind of watery, tasteless stew. As I toyed with my food, my fork speared a piece of greasy fat and I stared at it with nausea filling my throat. I passed the plate on to one of the others. Cat was there by my side to remind me, "You've got to eat, Baby."

But I couldn't.

When the so-called meal was finished, we were marched into a room no larger than a walk-in closet, where the twenty of us were lumped together to begin our processing. We were still in our jail issues and the room was cold. I couldn't help but laugh at the whole procedure—we were freezing our buns off with no panties or socks, much less jackets, and all they cared about was paperwork. I ached for a warm bed.

Mrs. O. was my first introduction to prison personnel. She entered the room, warned us to keep our mouths shut, and promptly handed out questionnaires to be filled in. Mrs. O. was black and looked like a snake ready to strike. She spoke in a monotone, as if she were bored with the whole affair, but there was a sharp edge to her voice as she constantly reminded us to keep our mouths shut. As she looked around the room, recognizing several inmates who were returnees, she became more talkative. "Well, well," she would ask sarcastically, "you just couldn't stay away, could you?" For those of us who were in prison for the first time, her beady little eyes glared at us and she had only sharp, rude remarks.

Once the forms had been completed, we were assigned seats and then Mrs. O. called each of us by name to her desk. As I stood there, an inmate poured disinfectant in my hair to kill head lice. Then Mrs. O. began going through the personal belongings I had brought with me. She determined what could be kept and what had to be returned. Anything you weren't allowed to keep had to be mailed home at personal expense. If you couldn't mail it, it was destroyed or designated for charity.

But I can assure you that very little was destroyed or sent to charity, because the inmates already in prison were like vultures—watching and snatching whatever they could lay their hands on. I had brought six pairs of snow-white panties with me, but they were trimmed in blue and were therefore against prison regulations, so Mrs. O. confiscated them. One of the other inmates ended up with them.

Our next checkpoint involved the issue of clothing. Our "white" jail issues were taken from us and we were issued prison "whites." It was really sort of humorous, in a twisted way. Here I was, convicted by a white jury, sentenced by a white judge, and driven to prison in a white bus. Now, to add further insult to my sensibilities, I could look forward to wearing nothing but white for the next twenty years. It seemed that all color was being removed from my life.

Next came the nurse's station for a physical examination. I was not opposed to this at all. After spending three months in the county jail, exposed to every disease in the world, I was anxious to be checked. I was not prepared, however, for the type of examination they provided. It was more humiliating and embarrassing than I can describe. I entered the room and was told to take my clothes off. Once I was undressed, the nurse told me to bend over the table and when I did, she rammed her finger up my rectum, searching for drugs.

Then I was made to lay down on the table with my legs spread. As I climbed up on the table, I could see only one speculum in the room and no sign of any means of sterilizing it. Before I could object, she grabbed the speculum and inserted it. I felt no lubrication, only a sharp, dry pain. I closed my eyes and once again, in spite of my promise just a few hours before, the tears began to flow. I was unable to control what was happening to me and my body.

Before the examination, I was afraid that I might have picked up some disease or germ at the county jail. Now I had to worry about picking up something from an unsterilized community speculum that was being used on, among others, the nineteen other women who had arrived with me.

After the examination, we were mercifully escorted to the showers where three of us at a time were allowed three minutes to wash our bodies and the disinfectant from our hair. I toweled off and for the first time put on my prison whites. I was clean, but I still felt dirty.

By two in the afternoon we had completed our "initial intake" process, but Mrs. O. had one more speech to deliver before we could be assigned to our cells. She glared at us for a minute and then sneered, "Listen up. You are now the property of the Texas Department of Corrections. As of this day, you are not Ms. Jane Doe but Ms. Jane Doe, T.D.C. #314036, or whatever number you have been assigned. Remember it. And when a guard calls out that number, it means you are to answer."

With that, the snake woman dismissed us and we were escorted to our individual cells.

Once inside, the prison door slammed shut, ringing with those familiar heavy metallic sounds we've all heard so many times on television and in the movies. As scary as it sounds on the screen, it is even more ominous and foreboding in real life. As those heavy barred doors slam shut and the keys are turned, locking you from the world, there is a finality about it that is numbing.

The air in the cell was heavy with the musty smell of urine, thinly concealed with a disinfectant. There was a bunk, a toilet bowl, a lock box, and a small water fountain and basin.

And there were roaches. Thousands of them. Everywhere I looked, the nasty things were running around—on the floor, up the walls, in and out of the toilet bowl.

But at last I was alone.

I was exhausted from the day, but I couldn't sleep. I simply stretched out on my bunk, a hard metal frame covered by a thin mattress, and my mind raced with thoughts of what was yet to come. What would it be like to live in "population," as the inmates called the prison. How was the family, especially Lee Jr. and Koquice, dealing with the knowledge that I was really in prison now? How many days or weeks would I have to stay here before Kerry won my appeal? I understood very little about appellate procedures at the time and had no idea that it would not move swiftly and surely to right an injustice. I certainly didn't expect the process to stretch into nine years.

3

Behind the Walls

Joyce Ann and I arrived at prison the same time, on the same chain. I'm sure she was scared to death; but she didn't show it. You could tell, though, that she was a time bomb waiting to explode. Other inmates could sense it and stayed out of her way. All it took was one look at Joyce and you knew this was one lady you didn't want to mess with. She was filled with self-pity. You could see her anger and hate; I tried to make her understand that there was only one way to do prison time: by not fighting it. I tried to make her understand, "You either do the time or the time will do you."

From day one, she fought the time. And she fought the system. Not physically, but mentally. She followed the rules and she did what she was told, but she didn't bend or allow herself to become anything other than what she felt herself to be—a temporary visitor who was in prison until her problem could be straightened out.

Almost everyone thought she was a real bitch—a stuck-up bitch who refused to become a part of the prison population. It was like there were two worlds:

the prison world and Joyce's world. But as bitchy and
as hateful as she was, people still wanted to be a part
of her world because when you looked past her bitter-
ness and hate, it was easy to see the strength of her
character. There was no one else like her in prison.
Joyce was a one of a kind.

–Katherlyn Shelley
Former Inmate, Goree Unit

Being exposed to the squalors of prison is humiliating enough when you're guilty of a crime, but being locked away like an animal for a crime you didn't commit is pure agony. Once you become a convict, prison officers cease to think of you as a human being and casually refer to you as a "liar," "a no good bitch," and "a piece of shit" not to be trusted.

Privacy becomes a thing of the past when you enter prison. You are housed with as many as thirty-four other women, most of whom are either thieves, murderers, baby killers, or con artists. You must learn to co-exist with society's outcasts in a living area about the size of a one-bedroom apartment that's equipped with four toilets, five showers, and one cubicle for all the inmates.

Everything you do, day and night, is under the watchful eye of a guard or your fellow inmates. Even the most intimate and private of personal hygienic attention is subject to scrutiny by someone. You are told when to get up, when to go to bed, when and for how long to eat, and when you can or cannot go to the bathroom. Every action is monitored and controlled by gray-uniformed guards who often give the impression that their sole mission in life is to remind you that you are no better than an animal. It is a way of life designed to break your spirit.

When I entered Goree I was confined, as are all new arrivals, to what is referred to as the Orientation Section. There, inmates are subjected to extensive interviews and medical tests. I especially remember the interview with the prison sociologist, a tall, heavy-set black woman. She stood well over six-feet tall and was a very imposing figure, but I was determined not to let her intimidate me in any way.

And she tried. She began by probing into every aspect of my life from childhood to the present, and she stressed over and over again that everything I told her would be checked out by T.D.C. If it was discovered that I had lied about anything, I would receive a "case" (be written up for disciplinary action) and as punishment could be assigned to segregation—the section not allowed to mingle with population. I assured her repeatedly that I didn't lie, period. When she began questioning me about every detail of the crime for which I had been convicted, I really got angry and yelled that I wasn't aware of any details because I had not committed the crime. She was persistent, but so was I. Fortunately, I only had to have one interview with her.

One of the most memorable things that took place during my stay in orientation occurred in the early hours of the morning, long after lights out, when everyone was asleep. I was awakened, as was everyone in my section, by the screams of a woman. Shocked, scared and very curious, we jumped up to see what was going on. My knuckles turned white as I gripped the bars of my cell, trying to figure out what was happening down the hall.

The screaming and moaning continued for several minutes and then there was a single, long screech of pain followed by several moments of complete silence. The silence was shattered by the sound of a slap. A second slap. Then we heard the sound of a newborn baby crying. We stood there in the dim light, glued to the bars, listening to the drama reaching our ears.

"What is that?"

"Who is that?"

"Who do you think it is?"

I didn't have to ask any questions. I knew what was going on and if it was going on in the dorm, it had to be illegal because pregnancies are handled at the Huntsville Hospital. I knew immediately that it would be my pleasure to blow the whistle on an illegal and clandestine birth within the prison. A guard came to our section and ordered us to shut up and get back to bed. But I didn't move. I was determined to get to the bottom of what was happening. I stood there for several minutes, straining my ears to catch any sound that might provide a clue to the early morning event. Then I heard a slight snicker,

followed by loud laughter. My smugness disappeared. We had been
suckered.

Big Doris, so named because her bras had to be special ordered
from the "free world" (outside prison), was housed in the dorm next
to the Orientation Section, and she took great pleasure in pulling her
little joke on all the new arrivals. For thirteen years, every newcomer
was introduced to life at Goree with Big Doris's "birth" of a baby.

During my stay at Goree, inmates were housed in wards and
cellblocks that were named after flowers and plants. In many instances, inmates convicted of similar crimes were retained in the same
ward. For example, all those who had killed a member of their family
were in one ward; inmates enrolled in the prison college courses were
kept in another ward; "Ivy Hall" was the home of the most
troublesome inmates; "Wisteria" was where many—though certainly
not all—lesbians, bulldaggers and stud broads lived. When I finally
was transferred to the general prison population I was assigned to
"Iris," a ward I assumed was for first offenders.

The beds were all double-bunks. New arrivals entering population
were automatically assigned to a top bunk. A lower bunk was not
only a status symbol, but a convenience. In an environment where
privileges were rare, a lower bunk was cherished and guarded. New
arrivals had to wait until someone was released, paroled, or transferred to another ward or unit before they could hope for a lower
bunk.

I'm very short, barely five feet tall, and it's quite an effort for me
to get in and out of a top bunk, so when I was told where I would be
sleeping, I really got pissed. I slammed my legal papers on the floor,
threw my carry-bags on top of the bed, and muttered some choice
words about the mother of the officer who had assigned me the bunk.
My behavior served as a convenient announcement to the fifty
women in the ward, "Don't fuck with me."

New arrivals are welcomed in prison, primarily because they
represent a departure from an extremely boring and uneventful norm.
When a new inmate enters a ward, she is greeted with all kinds of
questions from the inmates. My arrival was no different.

"Who are you?"

"What did you fall for?"

"How much time did you get?"

"Who was your attorney?"

These might seem like casual, politely-intentioned questions, but they are more than that. The answers fulfill an important social function within the prison system. The crime, the time, and the attorney are important topics of conversation as inmates discuss and compare their situations. There is a joke in prison that if you're low on cash in Texas, it's better to rob a convenience store than to forge checks. If you get caught and convicted for robbing a 7-Eleven, you'll get less time than if you bought something there with a hot check. And if you're sentenced for murder, "a nigger killing another nigger" will get far less time than "a nigger killing a white man." Two people who have committed identical crimes will get drastically different sentences, so inmates like to know their attorneys. Who is a good one? Who can get time cut? Who can get charges dropped or reduced? Who knows what he's doing? Who's not worth a shit?

When they started asking *me* all those questions, I just ignored them. What Martha Jean Bruce had done still burned inside me, and I was convinced that no inmate could be trusted. I wanted nothing to do with them. I wanted nothing to do with the staff. I just wanted to be left alone until I could get out and get back home to my family.

Soon after settling in, I was taken to the laundry to receive my full issue of state clothing. Ordinarily, inmates are issued jump-suits, but because of my large bust and small body, they couldn't find one that fit me. I was issued pants and shirts instead, plus a "rec" suit (for the one recreation session allowed during the entire three months I spent at Goree) and a skirt. All white, of course.

Everyone in prison works. Inmates are placed in work detail almost as soon as they move into the general population. When I was issued my clothing, I received my work assignment. It could have been worse. I could have been sent to the garment factory, where inmates make the officers' uniforms, or I could have been assigned to the laundry. I could have been sent to the fields to hoe weeds like a slave under the 110 degree Texas sun. I could have been sent out into the yard to mow grass, trim hedges, work in the flower beds, and keep the yard looking nice. Instead, I became a "key girl" in the prison infirmary.

My duties were simple. The locked door to the infirmary had a small glass pane. To gain admittance, an inmate was required to knock on the door and show a pass. As key girl, my job was to check the pass through the glass pane and then unlock the door. If I admitted anyone without an "official pass," I would be subject to disciplinary action from the officer or staff member in charge of the infirmary.

My job was easy, but the infirmary itself was a shock. I couldn't believe some of the things I saw going on. Inmates assigned to the infirmary were performing duties that I thought would have been administered only by a nurse or doctor. Inmates were allowed to take and record all vital signs, do pap smears, conduct blood tests, prepare lab cultures, take x-rays, and make entries on patients' charts and hospital records.

So what, you may ask, did the nurses do? As little as possible. They administered medications, but infirmary aides—considered to be the "chosen ones" because they were the pets of the infirmary staff— performed many medical functions. More than a few abused their status and power.

In fact, the "chosen ones" were so secure in their positions that they acted like officers. And an inmate who didn't know any better would even think they were officers. We knew that aides also had access to medicine, which they could obtain for themselves or for their friends. An inmate did not dare talk back or say anything derogatory to an aide. Doing so could result in a "case"—a disciplinary report—from an infirmary officer purely on the say-so of the infirmary aide, which meant punishment in the form of segregation. Some aides even used their position for profit; we even heard that some courted bribes from inmates to conceal medical conditions such as venereal disease.

While working as a key girl I met Granny, a legend at Goree. Granny was in her seventies when I arrived and had already served over twenty years for fatally poisoning her children and some of her grandchildren. She had come up for parole on several occasions, but the one surviving child—a son who had not gone to dinner that fateful night—refused to have her paroled into his custody. With no place to go, she was resigned to the fact that prison was her home for life. But because of her age and length of sentence, Granny more or less had the run of the prison and could come and go as she pleased.

One day, when a little old black woman with a cane knocked on the infirmary door I refused her admittance because she didn't have a pass. She knocked again, and again I looked through the pane but when I didn't see a pass, I ignored her. Several minutes later another inmate knocked on the door, displayed the appropriate pass, and I admitted her. She entered, followed by the strutting old woman. Before I could say a word, Granny cracked me over the head with her cane and said, "When Granny wants in, you let Granny in."

When Goree was closed down in the early '80s, Granny was moved to another unit. She had diabetes, was losing her sight, and shortly after being moved, one of her legs had to be amputated. From the day I met her, Granny always depressed me, even after her death in 1983. I used to have nightmares that I would end up like her—a shrivelled up little shell of a woman, wasting the rest of my days behind bars.

It didn't take the inmates long to discover that I was not someone they could take advantage of. One morning I was getting ready for work when I noticed that something was missing. I had arrived with several white nylon slips, trimmed in white lace. I treasured those slips. They were my link to better times, a better life. Nothing like them could be purchased at the commissary, and the only way to obtain such a prized item was to arrive with one, buy one from an individual, or steal it.

When I realized that someone had chosen the last option, I came unglued. I pitched a bitch they still talk about. In my nastiest voice, I let everyone in the ward know that I wanted my slip back *or else*. I yelled that if I had to, I would "snitch off" (go to the law) and demand a "shake" (a shakedown of each inmate's living quarters). "I'm going to work," I finally finished, "and when I get back tonight I want my slip on my bunk or there is going to be some hell around here."

I have always been a fighter. A fighter for my rights, my self-esteem, my property, my family, myself. When we were kids, my sister Mary would run from a fight. I would run *to* one if that's what it took to stand up for myself or my family. So at this stage in my life, I was not about to start my time by letting some thieving little witch rip me off. My dreams for Lee and Koquice had been shattered and my world had been brought to a screeching halt. Nothing seemed real anymore except the knowledge that I had to survive. That meant living from day to day and doing whatever I had to do to get me through. And believe me, there were times when I was so hurt, so humiliated, that I wanted to crawl away and die. I had to just physically shake myself, like a dog shakes off bugs or water, in order to get the weak thoughts out of my head. I would think of my family. What would they think of me if I gave up? That's why I fought for my slip.

There is a lie perpetuated by movies, television shows, and books that there is "honor among thieves." Forget that bull. The people in prison would steal your false teeth if you left them laying around—unless they knew there would be repercussions. Fear is what "honor among thieves" is all about. When I returned that evening, my slip was folded neatly on the foot of my bunk.

That incident pretty well established my reputation as someone not to be messed with. Cat, who was still looking out for me in spite of my attitude, aided my cause by telling everyone, "That lady is a fool, she's crazy. You don't want to get her started. Leave her alone." After that incident, though, she pulled me aside. "Baby, you got to keep your cool. If you start off fighting, you'll end up doing your sentence fighting, not only with everyone in sight, but you'll be fighting time, too." She added, "That will only make it rougher on you."

"I don't care," I told her. I didn't care what a bunch of inmates or guards thought of me. I wasn't completely alone, anyway. Cat stood by me, and there were other inmates, mostly new arrivals like myself, who clung to me because I seemed strong.

I found out later that a little fat Mexican bitch had stolen my slip for her homosexual lover or, as they say in prison, her "people."

I was not prepared for the boldness of homosexuals in the prison community, nor was I prepared for the extent of their lifestyle. As I mentioned earlier, when I first entered population I was subjected to a lot of curious questions. In addition to the usual ones, there were a few unusual ones, like, "Joyce, do you have people?"

The first time I was asked if I had "people," naturally I thought I was being asked about my family. Happy to talk about the one subject that really interested me, I went into a proud description of my babies, my mama, and my brothers and sisters. Later I found out that I had a lot to learn about prison language. All the lesbians weren't in Wisteria Hall, so I had to flat out let everyone know that I didn't have no people and I wasn't interested in having any.

I especially remember two white girls who lived in my ward. Kathy, who was a short, fat blonde, readily admitted she had been a lesbian for as long as she could remember. The other one, Susan, a masculine woman with a terrible skin complexion, displayed a jail-induced preference for women. One night, long after lights out, I overheard these two "stud-broads" (lesbians with masculine behavior) talking about me.

Susan, who slept on the bunk beneath mine, finally whispered out, "Joyce! Joyce!"

I pretended I was asleep.

"Joyce, I know you're not asleep," Susan added.

Silence.

Kathy asked, "Why are you so mean? Why won't you talk to us? We've never done anything to you."

Something inside me snapped. Before I knew it I was spitting out my feelings in one long, fiery breath. I told them the entire story, from the time I was arrested, through Martha Jean Bruce lying about me, to when I was convicted and sent here.

When I finally finished, there was a long silence. Then Susan whispered softly, "I'm sorry."

Still mad, I snapped back, "Thanks, but sorry won't get me out of here."

They told me a little about themselves, and then Kathy asked me the inevitable question, "Do you play around, Joyce?"

"Not unless you have a bat and two balls."

She burst out laughing, and even I joined with them. For the briefest moment we were just three kids away from home, whispering in the dark.

But one of our "parents" heard us laughing and barked, "Alright, ladies, lights are out! It's time for bed! Get quiet back there!"

We peered down the hallway and saw that it was the guard we called "The Campbell Soup Kid," because she looked like the kid on the commercial. We all burst out laughing again.

The Campbell Soup Kid left her desk and walked back in our direction and said, "I'm giving you ladies an order. Get quiet!"

Susan screamed out, "Fuck off!"

The guard couldn't figure out who had screamed, and luckily she went back to her post and left us alone. Kathy and Susan fell asleep, but I lay in the quiet darkness wondering how many more nights I would spend on this bunk. Someone, somewhere soon would admit that a mistake had been made. Any day now they would call my name and tell me I was going home.

4

Welcome to Mountain View

I met Joyce in 1981 at the Goree Unit, and from the moment of our very first meeting I became a Joyce Ann Brown supporter and friend. When you're locked up in prison, you hear many inmates claiming to be innocent. Most of the time it's best to just nod your head and agree with them, even though you know inside they're guilty as hell.

But from the moment I met Joyce, I knew she was innocent. She didn't have to tell me. I just knew. And from 1981, I never changed my mind. In all those years, I watched Joyce, and she never changed. She was stronger than most, had more character than most, and was more giving than most.

During her first year in prison, Joyce was different from the others. She didn't try to make friends, but inmates came to her wanting to be her friend. It was as if she was the queen and we were her subjects—but she wasn't aware of it. She was simply Joyce.

–Gloria
Inmate, MountainView Unit

On March 26, 1981, while working in the infirmary, one of the aides showed me a memo from the Mountain View unit. It was a request for the medical records of a number of inmates. Such a request always signalled that transfers were coming up. As I looked over the list, one of the names jumped out at me—mine. I was being transferred to Mountain View, a maximum security state prison for women in Gatesville, Texas.

I sat at my desk. It had been five months since the trial. What was ahead now? Instead of moving closer to freedom, I seemed to be sinking deeper and deeper into the state's penitentiary system.

The system struck out at me again by separating me from Cat, the one person I had come to care about in those halls of gloom. From the day I landed in the county jail, Cat had always been there—smiling, laughing, calming me down. Now I had to leave her behind.

On the morning of my transfer I was up early. I neatly packed all my belongings in my "chain bags." These are simply the bright red mesh bags used at produce markets for vegetables and fruits, but we used them for suitcases. Since they are the fifty-pound size, you can pack quite a bit of stuff in them. But it was a waste of time to pack, because as soon as I was through, the Inventory Officer came around, made me dump everything out on the floor, and did a shake. When she was finished, I packed everything again. At 9:00 a.m. I was told to report to the check-out point downstairs.

When I arrived downstairs, my spirits lifted because Cat was standing there smiling. I had a quick happy thought that maybe her name had been added to the list at the last moment and was pulling chain with me. But she had only come to say good-bye.

"Why aren't you coming with me?"

"Mountain View is a maximum security unit, J.B. I'll be leaving here too, but I'll probably get sent to Riverside."

Cat was in jail for writing bad checks, so she was going to Riverside, a minimum security prison. The only way she would make it to Mountain View was if she got "the bitch" thrown at her, and of course I couldn't wish that on her.

The bitch is the Habitual Criminal Act, which enables any district attorney to incarcerate a person for life if that person has two or more prior convictions for the same offense. A district attorney can throw the bitch at any defendant with three or more convictions. It's used most often as a bartering tool. If you don't comply with a D.A.'s request for information or testimony, he can literally lock you up and throw away the key. That's why there are so many people serving twenty-five years or more in maximum security prisons for petty crimes. Cat had been convicted several times for writing hot checks, but luckily no one had used the bitch on her.

Cat and I stood there, holding each other, crying, promising to write. Then those of us pulling chain began boarding the bus. Within a few minutes we were pulling out, and I watched my friend grow smaller and smaller as we drove away. It was the last time I saw Cat.

As we headed for Mountain View, I couldn't help but smile. Cat had managed to "get over the man" again. Everyone in prison has a way of fighting back against the system, and Cat had just done it. Getting over the man means pulling a fast one and getting away with it, or breaking a rule and not getting caught.

Cat was notorious for her antics. Simply being there to see me off was a classic example. Somehow she had conned her way into the check-out point, despite the fact that if the guards had discovered she was "out of place" (being somewhere without a pass), she would have faced a severe disciplinary case.

Sitting on the bus, I remembered the first time Cat involved me in one of her little incidents. One Saturday afternoon, we had each been on a visit with our families. After visiting hours, we went together to the dining room for lunch. All the other inmates had eaten and the dining room was empty except for the clean-up crew. There was still quite a bit of chicken left on the steam table, so Cat decided we should boost some. I went along with the idea and put a little extra chicken on my tray, but as we were eating, I noticed she had a *bundle* on the seat next to her. I knew immediately what the bundle was and that if we were caught with it, we'd be in deep shit. I murmured, "How do you expect to get that out of here?"

Cat smiled and answered. "We're gonna leg it."

"Legging it" involves concealing the goods in your panties, between your legs. That's how contraband is moved around within the prison. Since I was wearing a skirt, I knew I had been elected to do the legging. Somehow, sitting the middle of the cafeteria, I managed to get that bundle—wrapped in a stolen dish towel—down my panties and between my legs. Have you ever tried to walk with a bundle of hot chicken cooking your privates? I wobbled out of the dining room, trying to look nonchalant. We made it to the stairs before a guard noticed something peculiar about me. "Hey you!" she yelled.

I could have waited to see if maybe she was talking to someone else, but instead I turned the corner and took the stairs two at a time, dropping drumsticks every which way as I ran back to the ward. That night, Cat and I had a midnight snack: the best-tasting chicken I ever had in my life.

The bus ride from Goree to Mountain View took about three and a half hours, but I can't recall any of the scenery. I had already checked out the inmates pulling chain with me and had quickly decided none of them were the kind of people I wanted anything to do with. So I buried myself in thought. I wrapped myself in my hatred like a winter coat. While the others were joking and clowning around, I sat there nursing my feelings of disgust.

After an hour or so, the inmate handcuffed to me turned and asked, "Are you all right?"

I glared right through her and didn't answer. She turned away and we continued to ride in silence. The other inmates saw what happened and they all got real quiet. I could feel their eyes on me and could hear their whispers. "She's mean." "She's crazy." I didn't care. I didn't want them to like me. That way I wouldn't be bothered.

When we arrived at Mountain View, the bus stopped to allow the guard to open the large electronically controlled front gate. Once inside, we filed off the bus and were hustled off to Classification for assignment to jobs and housing. One of the inmates chained up with me, Twenty-Grand, asked me, "Where will you be working?"

When I answered, her mouth flew open in disbelief. I had been assigned to work as a clerk, which was considered a real privilege. I, however, have never been able to see it that way. The fact that I was required to work for no pay when I could be out working and making money was not my idea of a privilege. I resented it with all my being.

Next I was escorted to my new "house," C-2 Dorm. The dorms were separated by a "pipe chase," an area where the duty officer is stationed in order to observe both sides of the dorm. When the officer opened the door, I went inside and was greeted by three inmates who offered to help me with my bags. I wasn't met by the usual questions. Instead they simply asked, "What bed you got?" Then I realized why they weren't interested in my crime or my time. Inmates were whispering in the background.

"That's her."

"No it ain't."

"Yes it is. That's her."

Finally, Rosalinda, a tall, healthy-looking black woman asked, "Ain't you that gal that Martha Bruce went back to Dallas and lied on?"

My God, I thought. Here I was in a roomful of people who knew Martha Bruce had framed me.

"Yes," I answered. "I'm that gal. I'm Joyce."

Pointing to the third bed in the dorm, Rosalinda said, "That old bitch slept right there."

I shrugged my shoulders. That's all I needed. A constant reminder of Martha Jean Bruce, right where I could see it every day.

Rosalinda stayed with me, helping me get squared away in the three-by-six-foot cubicle that was my new house. She was what we call "cornbread fed," real country. And she was loud. I found out soon enough that she had a reputation of being "messy," the word used to describe someone who always keeps some kind of shit brewing among inmates, brewing it to such a point that trouble—and a little excitement for Rosalinda—develops. She was a "story-carrier," taking tales from one inmate to another about who was two-timing on her people or who was doing this or that. She also was no dummy. I kept my distance from her because I knew she could be trouble. Being a new inmate on the unit and anticipating going home at any time, I kept hearing what Kerry Fitzgerald had told me in our last meeting: "Kid, stay out of trouble and keep your nose clean."

After I had stored my things away, I went to the pipe chase for my toilet articles. The officer handed out soap, toothpowder, and toilet tissue. In those days, we were issued a large bar of pretty green soap with the Texas State Seal on it, but today they have cut it down to a small white bar just a little bit bigger than complimentary motel soap.

Since the Ruiz ruling in 1985, the state has made a lot of similar reductions and cutbacks. At one time, indigents (inmates not receiving outside help from family or friends) were given shampoo, lotions, toothpaste, sanitary pads, deodorant, and tobacco shavings donated by various tobacco companies which could be rolled into cigarettes. That generous policy has been discontinued and today, if an inmate doesn't receive money from the outside to purchase these necessities, she has to do without. Thank God I had money from my family and friends. And since I have never smoked, I didn't have to waste my precious allowance on that habit.

Fortunately, the state still provides inmates with sanitary napkins. When I first arrived, the unwrapped and not-so-sanitary napkins and tampons were stored in large, open boxes. When an inmate needed them, she had to go to the guard and ask for her monthly supply (24 napkins and tampons, 12 of each). If an inmate needed more than that, a note from the infirmary was required. No note, no napkins. Today, sanitary napkins are individually wrapped and more hygienic, but the policy concerning them is still primitive. Like children asking for candy, inmates still have to ask politely for their monthly supply.

Nor has the policy changed concerning women who endure a hard time during their monthly cycle. Work is still required and no exceptions are made unless one has a medical lay-in (an excused absence from duty) from the infirmary. However, a lay-in is never issued to women simply for having a period. So if your cramps are so bad you can't do your work, you have to lie and fake another illness.

At any rate, once I was issued my toilet articles, I returned to my cubicle, which was equipped with a plastic chair, a wooden desk, an iron bed with a thin mattress, a metal gallon trash can, and a lock box attached to the head of the bed. Surprisingly, rest came easily that first night in C-2 Dorm. I went to sleep, determined that no matter what challenges came up the next day, I could deal with them.

The following morning I reported to my new job at 8:00 a.m. to begin a two week training period as a secretary. My supervisor was Lieutenant K. He was a tall, slim redneck and many of the inmates joked about how "fine and desirable" he was. "That white man can park his shoes under my bed *any*time." "You tell Lt. K. he can come visit me anytime he wants to." "Tell that white bastard he ain't lived until he's had *me*."

The only thing about Lt. K. that interested me was the ring he wore on his finger. Across the face of it were the initials "KKK." If I had to work with the man, I wanted to know if those initials meant what I thought they meant. After a few tactful inquiries, I discovered that they were actually the initials of his full name. When he finally left T.D.C. in 1984, though, he was still believed by many to be a member of the Klan.

To me, Lt. K. was disgusting. He chewed tobacco and had spit cans scattered all over the office floor. He took great delight in target practice, spitting into those cans from a distance of ten or fifteen feet. He especially enjoyed performing his nasty little practice when one of the inmates was standing near one of his spit cans. When I first saw him take aim and let it fly, I knew that if he ever spit on me we were going to touch the four walls of that office fighting. I couldn't stand his nasty habit.

There was another nasty practice I couldn't stand. It was a certain embellishment on the shake-down policy. As an inmate, no matter what you are doing and no matter where you are, you must submit to a shake from any guard any time of the day or night. This involves standing at attention while a guard rubs her hands all over your body, searching for illegal and concealed contraband. Many officers, familiar with the inmate practice of legging it, delight in giving a sharp chop of their hand to your crotch.

There are some officers who are polite, in their way, in conducting a standard and routine check of your body. And there are some who pretend to be friendly and try to put a con on you. They might greet you with something like, "Good evening, Joyce. How are you today?"

Was I civil back? Hell no! I recognized the little game they were playing. These were the ones who didn't give a damn about your feelings. The minute you walked away, they would turn to a fellow guard or inmate and say, "I can't stand that stuck-up bitch. She thinks her shit don't stink." The only reason they are polite is because they have been ordered by the warden to be more courteous to the inmates and, oh, do they resent having to treat us with respect.

I, in turn, resented their phoniness and I really resented the chops to the crotch. That's one of the reasons I always wore a skirt as often as possible. I found that even the most insensitive guards are reluctant to "chop the crotch" when you're wearing a skirt.

In 1981, the Mountain View Unit had a completely different environment and atmosphere than it does today. Back then, there weren't as many women in prison and there were eight dorms, A through H. All were minimum-custody dorms, where security was not very rigid. E Dorm, home of the "warden's girls," was even more relaxed. These favorites either worked for the warden or for some other reason were considered by her to deserve special treatment. They enjoyed more freedom than the rest of us, including unlocked doors twenty-four hours a day, and they could come and go as they pleased without a pass. E Dorm girls did their own "head count" every morning and night and called the total to the count officer. It was even forbidden for officers to write them up with a disciplinary case without the warden's express approval. When Warden Plain retired in 1986 and the effects of the Ruiz Ruling began to circulate, E Dorm was renovated into what it is now, Death Row.

I lived in C Dorm for several weeks before being moved to H Dorm. H Dorm housed inmates who were not considered "problems" for prison officers. Any inmate with a case or disciplinary action could not be moved into or remain in H Dorm. Consequently, I welcomed the move. H Dorm inmates seemed like a different breed of ladies, who showed more respect for each other and the officers. We also enjoyed a few extra advantages, such as less harassment from officers and slightly less supervision.

A few days after moving in I was walking to the dining room, deuced up (walking in pairs) with my new dormmates. As we passed some of the other inmates, I overheard a girl named Dorothy say to an inmate standing next to her, "Well, well, well, look at H Dorm, the baby-killing bitches."

I didn't know what she was talking about and turned to Breezy, the lady I was deuced with. "Why is she calling us baby killers? Is that what you're in for?"

Breezy shook her head and said, "No, honey, I ain't no baby killer. Don't pay no attention to her." Then she added, "But most of the women in our dorm are in prison for killing their kids."

I was too shocked to speak. And too repulsed to even look at the food before me. Baby killers! I was living with women who could take the life of an innocent child. There seemed to be no limit to the depravity of this place.

And then it was Christmas.

5

The Art of Survival

Late one night in 1982, while I was at the Women's Diagnostic Unit, I was listening to some ladies talk. They were in the cell directly across the hall from my cell, and this woman, Rene Taylor, was talking about her case. She said that she had received a life sentence for robbery and murder. When someone asked her where she fell from, she answered, "Dallas." Then she proceeded to say that she hoped T.D.C. did not send her to Mountain View. Since I knew that unit was the nicest and best of all the women's units, I asked her why she didn't want to go there.

"Because Joyce Ann Brown is there doing time for the same crime. She wasn't even there. It was someone else."

I asked Rene why she didn't just go ahead and clear the Brown woman and she answered, "The girl that did do it with me has a family to take care of. And I am not going to take her away from all of that."

–Kathy Carpentier
Former Inmate

Summer passed, and then autumn. December came with no change of heart from Rene and no word of an appeal or retrial. As I lay in bed on the twenty-fourth of that month, I prepared for my first Christmas away from home. The next morning, Lee and Koquice would open their presents under someone else's tree. My family and friends would gather for dinner without me. But if I could just make it through the day, I promised myself, I would never have to endure Christmas in prison again. I resolved to spend the next day sleeping, shutting off, ignoring everyone. When you're asleep, you don't hurt.

Christmas morning dawned with those awake pulling the bunks of those asleep out into the halls, waking them up for breakfast. They pulled my bed out and woke me up, but I refused to go down to the dining hall. I got up and parked myself in front of the television set, watched the parades, and waited for the football game to begin.

That evening, they started in on me again. Everyone wanted me to go down for Christmas dinner. But the last thing I intended to do was march down to the dining hall, eat dinner, sing Christmas songs, and fake having a good time with a bunch of people I barely knew.

To me, it wasn't Christmas. Even the traditional symbols of Christmas were almost non-existent. Only caroling and token decorations like a tiny tree in the dayroom were allowed. Christmas parties and dancing were forbidden. Inmates were not even allowed to have a radio in the dayroom for playing Christmas music. Except for the large Christmas tree in the dining hall and the Salvation Army visit at night, Christmas in prison was just another day.

But those women were determined. They pressed me to come along to the service, explaining that the Salvation Army would be there passing out gifts and goodies to all the inmates; but to receive the presents, you had to attend the service. I could have cared less. I just wanted to be alone. But then one inmate said that attendance was a way of showing appreciation to the Salvation Army volunteers. Another added, "Joyce, think of someone other than yourself. Those people didn't have to come visit us on Christmas day, but they want us to know that someone other than our family cares."

So I went. And I knew it was a mistake the minute I entered the dining hall. A group of inmates were singing Christmas songs and the sound of their voices immediately brought back memories of home. These were songs I had always sung with my family. Somehow I made it through the food line—others put the food on my tray—and then I made it to the table where I sat, without eating, trying to ignore everything around me. There was a Christmas tree, of course, but I can't remember what it looked like. I do remember the harsh, bright glare of the overhead lights and how they made the Santa's faded and dingy beard look even more drab against his pale skin. The goodies and gifts passed out by the Salvation Army people sat untouched in front of me. I just stared straight ahead, wondering what my Lee and Koquice were doing at that moment, whether they had enjoyed a good Christmas, whether they missed their mother as much as I missed them.

I had cried so much already I felt for once I was going to make it through the ordeal without shedding a tear, but as someone passed behind me I heard a voice say, "That's Joyce Brown. I feel real sorry for her. She didn't do anything."

It just kept happening. People kept saying they felt sorry for me, that I shouldn't be in prison. But I was, and there was nothing I could do about it except listen to that quiet voice that kept telling me, "God has not forsaken you." Then the Salvation Army folks began to sing:

Silent night, holy night
All is calm, all is bright.

It was more than I could handle. The hurt within me burst out, and I cried from rage, from pain, from frustration. I lost all thought of maintaining my composure. As I sat there on that cold hard seat, arms folded on the table, head buried in my arms, I cursed the system that had taken me away from my children. I cursed the white bastards who had looked at me and had seen only "another nigger" to send to jail. I cried and cursed because I was crying and cursing. I had lost it.

But I vowed then and there I would never lose it again. I was Joyce Ann Brown and I was innocent.

Throughout the following year, each day was a carbon copy of the one before. I slept, ate, went to work, and lived for mail and visits from my family. Kerry had warned me that an appeal would take several months, and inmates laughingly said it would never happen so quick. But every morning I woke up thinking that maybe today was the day.

There was a brief moment of hope when Rene Taylor, friend of the Joyce Ann Brown in Denver, was captured in Detroit, Michigan. She confessed to both the robbery and the murder of Mr. Danziger, but would not reveal the name of her accomplice. Rene too was now housed at Mountain View. Soon after her arrival, another inmate pointed her out to me in the hall, but I was unable to approach her. The authorities were under strict order to keep us separated, and they were careful never to place us in the same room or general area together.

Living under the same roof with the person who had the information that could free me, but who refused to reveal it, was maddening. It only added to the bitterness already festering inside me. If there was anything positive about my attitude during those months, it was that it was non-discriminatory. I disliked, mistrusted, and avoided most blacks as well as most whites. To suggest I was suffering more than they were would be foolish, because I am sure I was not alone with my frustrations and disappointments. But I was so wrapped up in my own pain that I had no idea how others were coping. I only knew I hated it.

That hatred was beginning to control not only my thoughts, but my behavior as well. One day I realized that it was beginning to infect my family, too. At that time, Lee Jr. was living with his paternal grandmother and wasn't able to visit as often as Koquice, but MaDear arranged to bring him along whenever possible. Since my imprisonment, I had been trying to encourage, caution, and advise them in all matters during those brief moments the state allowed for visiting time. On their holiday visit just after Thanksgiving, Koquice made a comment that I couldn't get out of my mind.

We had been talking about the delays in my request for an appeal, and Koquice just broke down. "I hate them, Mama! I hate all of them! And I hate those stupid laws that put you here!"

I tried to calm her down. "You mustn't hate them, Koquice. They were just trying to do their job." But how could I convincingly persuade my daughter not to hate when her mother was filled with it herself?

Christmas of 1982 was celebrated with the same dreary traditions as the year before, but this time I noticed something. In spite of the circumstances, a spirited sense of sisterly love did manage to prevail among the inmates. For once in the year, everyone showered good will upon each other. Inmates who could afford it contributed something for the dayroom buffet, such as cookies, candies, cakes, and other snacks. They would also exchange small gifts, especially contraband items like cream or "gold" (sugar). Inmates are not allowed to have gold because homebrew or "hooch" can be made from it. And yes, some inmates did make hooch. It's made from yeast, sugar, water and some kind of fruit, such as raisins, oranges, watermelon, or grapes. All the ingredients are mixed together and allowed to sit in a dry area for two or three weeks where it "cooks" to its full potency. When the alcohol is ready, it's mixed with fruit juice or punch to create a potent beverage.

It was within this atmosphere of determined rejoicing that I began to really take a good look at myself. I watched the inmates laughing and singing, opening their modest gifts, sneaking sips of hootch out of paper cups, and something dawned on me. These inmates were human too. I had something in common with them and I wanted to touch them. If I was going to stay human and walk out of prison feeling good about myself, it was time for a change.

That night in my cell, I knelt beside my bunk and talked to God. To be a decent mother, I had to let go of the anger and hatred. I asked God to fill my heart with love, to replace the bitterness with compassion, and to erase all my hostility. I would need all the strength I could muster to make that gut-wrenching adjustment: Until my innocence could be proven, I was a convicted felon living in a penitentiary. Period. It was time to accept that and move on. Before I went to sleep, I made out a list of New Year's resolutions. At the top of that list was the promise to become, once again, the person my mama had taught me to be.

The following Saturday, I started where Mama always started— with her house. Dorms might appear to be clean and neat, but they aren't. Superficial cleaning and straightening up is conducted only to appease the officers on their regular cursory inspections. In those early years, there was a "Clean Dorm Contest" every six months, promising "free world cake, cookies, and punch" to the residents with the cleanest dorm. But it was common knowledge that the prize was actually stale cookies and watered-down punch from the kitchen. So it was almost impossible to get inmates enthusiastic about the idea of "deep-cleaning" the "house."

There is a great lack of pride, self-esteem, and self-respect among inmates behind prison walls. The boredom, tedium, and self-pity create an atmosphere of laziness, an attitude of "what the hell, it doesn't matter." This atmosphere and attitude is mirrored in the way many of the inmates live. Their laziness and lack of pride extends to their "houses."

I decided not to be a victim of either the atmosphere or the attitude. I couldn't do anything about the drabness of prison, but from Mama I knew I could do something about the filth. I resolved that my house would be cleaned, and cleaned not just every six months, but as often as necessary.

So that Saturday morning I woke up early, went into the dayroom, unplugged the television set, and moved it into the clothing room where it was out of sight and unavailable. Next, I went to the officer on duty and talked her out of some cleaning materials. Then, with an old toothbrush, vinegar, rags, and shampoo, I got down on my knees and began to clean the dayroom floor.

After a few minutes of vigorous cleaning, one of the inmates ventured into the dayroom. "Joyce, what are you doing?"

"I'm cleaning this pigsty up," I answered. "And no matter how long it takes, there will be no television until I'm finished."

In a New York minute, half the women in the dorm filled the dayroom area to join me. They attacked the windows with rags and wads of old newspaper. With all their help, the job didn't take long. Once everyone was working together, I went outside the dorm into the hall, and brought back a water hose and some bottles of detergent. Then I sudsed and rinsed the entire area down from top to bottom, wall to wall. I sprayed the ceiling and walked down the dayroom aisle with the water hose, followed by two other inmates who swept out the water with brooms.

While all this was going on, I could hear the girls in their cubicles giggling and laughing, teasing me with the old wive's tale about how "crazy people like to play in the water." I just smiled and continued cleaning that place like there was no tomorrow.

After the floor had dried, I gave it the finishing touch.

It was another trick I learned from MaDear and one that created a little bit of a mystery among the officers. None of them could figure out what we did to the floors to make them so shiny. It was really quite simple. I rubbed the floor with baby oil. Baby oil gives a cement floor a shine and lustre that's unbelievable—so much so that you can see your reflection in the floor when it's applied properly. When the work was done, the women marveled at what they had accomplished.

The officers raved. We achieved the reputation of having the cleanest house on the block and won the "Clean Dorm" contest several times and tied for it several more. More importantly, the combined efforts of everyone in our dorm created a togetherness and sense of well-being that comes from a job well done. And it gave us all a clean place to live.

Next, I tackled my job situation. I didn't mind working myself to death keeping my house clean, but it still galled me to have to work without any compensation. In my job as a Support Services Inmate (or secretary), I was required to work around fifty-six hours a week. So when I learned through the prison grapevine that a job in the gym was opening up, I went for it. Aides in the gym do all the mopping, sweeping and cleaning up after recreation hours, and although the work isn't easy, it involves only a few hours a day. That was the job for me.

First I talked to Cal, a gym aide I knew slightly. When I explained that I wanted to work with her, she was perfectly agreeable. In fact, she said that if I would do all the paperwork in the gym office, she would do the cleaning. Sounded great to me. Only two problems remained. First, I had to convince the Major to let me transfer, and then I had to talk the gym supervisor into giving me the job.

When I stepped into the Major's office and announced I wanted a transfer, she looked at me with astonishment. Why would one of her girls want to leave?

"So I can be transferred to the gym," I explained.

Shaking her head in disbelief, she asked, "Joyce, are you aware of how much work is involved down there?"

"Yes, Ma'am."

"Are you aware of the birds?"

"The birds?" She had me there. I had not heard about the birds.

"The birds get inside the gym, make a mess on the bleachers, and the aides have to clean it up."

"Major," I began to explain as earnestly as possible, "you know I'm not afraid of work and I'm sure not afraid of working in the gym. But I need this transfer. I'm bogged down. My mind is playing tricks on me. I need a new job or I'm going to explode."

She studied me for such a long time that I started to get nervous. "Major, are you angry with me for wanting a transfer?"

She laughed. "Joyce Ann, if I get mad you'll know it. If I ever give you a job change to the yard, laundry, or kitchen for no reason then you'll know the Major is angry with you."

Relieved, I pushed on. "Major, I need a change. I really do."

She dismissed me with, "I'll think about it and let you know."

I left her office feeling a little less than confident, but figured I had nothing to lose by going right to the job source. I walked over to the Educational and Recreational building and went in to see the gym supervisor, Mr. S. I didn't beat around the bush. "Mr. S., I understand you're looking for a new aide to work in the gym."

"Uh-huh," he answered, never looking up from his work.

"Well, I want the job," I informed him.

He looked up at me with a big smile and said, "Ms. Brown, it's a lot of work."

I almost laughed because I knew he knew it was really a cushy job, so I realized he had already talked to the Major. "I can handle it, sir."

He continued. "I could use a good worker, but I want you to know there's quite a bit to deal with at the gym."

I didn't care what had to be dealt with. I wanted the job and kept after him to arrange for my transfer. And I got it. I went from working fifty-six hours a week down to about seventeen. I was learning the art of survival in prison.

There were other lessons to be learned in this art, as I soon discovered. The art of choosing friends, for instance. You have to do it *very* carefully. My new co-worker Slick taught me this one.

Slick also worked in the Educational and Recreational building. When I first went to work for Mr. S., Slick learned she would have to take some time off for surgical stay at John Sealy Medical Center, the T.D.C. hospital. She was afraid that she might lose her job while she was gone and be reassigned to a less favorable position—perhaps even to the yard. Since I knew her pretty well from the E&R building and also from my dorm, I agreed to work my job and hers. Until she returned from the hospital, I would do my job in the morning and cover for her in the afternoon.

The arrangement worked fairly well, although I was anxious to resume my short day duties. Finally, Slick returned from her surgery, but then I agreed to continue working for her until she regained her strength. That's when I learned *again* that in prison you have to be very careful.

Fifty stamps were stolen from a security officer's desk in the E&R building where Slick worked. Fortunately for me, it was my commissary day, so I had not been required to work the day the stamps were stolen. The security officer, Mrs. T., immediately called the mail room and told them to be on the alert for any letters bearing the particular missing stamps. Inmates are only allowed to purchase stamps from the Commissary, and the stamps are all identical. The stolen stamps had been purchased in the free world and had a different pattern.

I had no idea of what was going on until I returned from the commissary and was met outside the E&R building by Slick.

"Joyce, I need your help," she said, panic in her eyes.

"Sure, Slick," I replied, wondering what was up.

"I boosted some stamps from Mrs. T.'s desk and I think she knows it was me. I need you to go in my house, get those stamps out of my locker, and hold them for me."

I reluctantly agreed, but as I walked toward the dorm, I began to experience some conflicting doubts. There are so many acts and codes in prison. One requires you to look out for a friend; but another requires you to look out for yourself. If I had been caught with those stamps, I would have been in deep trouble. And although Slick was supposedly a friend, I wasn't sure she wouldn't deny the whole thing and finger me to keep herself out of trouble. In the end, I retrieved the stamps, but rather than holding them for her, I dropped them in the trash can.

Sure enough, the mail room people discovered several envelopes bearing the missing stamps, and they were on letters written by Slick. About fifteen minutes after I had grabbed the stamps from Slick's house, the guards showed up and staged a shakedown of her quarters. Since the stamps weren't there, Slick was able to beat the rap by claiming the stamps she had used were recycled—used stamps that were not postmarked. Without recovering the missing stamps, they couldn't prove Slick was the actual thief.

I later heard that my house had also been initially included for a shake, but they dropped the idea when they learned I had not worked the day the stamps were taken.

That evening when Slick returned from work, I told her, "They searched your house."

"Do you have the stamps?" she wanted to know.

And I told her, "No, I threw them in the trash."

Then she had the nerve to ask me to retrieve the stamps and go with her to drop them where they would be found by another inmate. Her idea was for someone else to use the stamps, so that when the mail room saw them the heat would be transferred from Slick onto someone else.

You can imagine my reply.

For several days afterward, Slick treated me like I was wearing the snitch jacket, though I had actually helped her out more than she deserved. We never were friends again after that, which didn't bother me in the least.

Stealing is common behind the walls, and no one is exempt from the swift fingers of a thief. Whites steal from blacks, blacks steal from whites, whites and blacks steal from each other, and all boosters steal from the staff. They steal because they need it, because they want it, and often just for the hell of it. Some would steal the white out of rice.

In the end, Slick paid for her crime. She was fired from her job and reassigned to a less privileged position. Her misfortune taught me a valuable lesson: in prison, take care of yourself *first*.

However, her misfortune turned out to be mine too, because I was given her job. Suddenly, my seventeen-hour work week was more than doubled. But there was a positive side. Working two jobs in the E&R building, I came in contact with a wide range of personalities every day, including inmates, staff, and people from the free world. I met sad and abused people who had given up on life; I met illiterates struggling to learn and better themselves; I met "short timers," "lifers," and many who had no business being in prison at all; but most importantly, I met most of the prison personnel members and began to learn that not all gray suits (officers) or civilian staff members are racist, uncaring, and unconcerned. Some of them are very warm and caring human beings.

Mr. S., who was in charge of both education and recreation, was the first to earn my respect and, later, my affection. I can honestly testify that I have never met a finer gentleman in all my life. Mr. S. is a God-fearing man, always available to discuss a personal problem and ready with a solution or another way to look at it. He treats everyone, inmates and staffers, with respect and never issues demeaning orders or commands. He may well be the kindest and most understanding man in the Texas prison system. Mr. S. has only one weakness. He is constantly going on diets—and breaking them. The poor man is forever trying to get down to 190 pounds. In the six years I worked for him, he never reached his goal.

And there is Madame Butterfly.

When we were told that a security officer's job was opening up and that Madame Butterfly wanted it, the E&R aides went into a panic. We were sure she would upset our regular routine of cushy hours and little perks, which we would go to any measure to protect. Paramount among our concerns was the fact that we all worked near the teacher's lounge. Why was that a factor? Because that's where there was always a pile of free world cookies, cake, and fresh glazed donuts available to any inmate willing to display a little initiative. For instance, volunteering to fetch coffee for a staff member just naturally involved passing the goodie table where a quick pair of hands could boost a donut or two, maybe even a pocketful of cookies. I have to smile when I think of how many times I would jump from my desk and tell Mr. S. or Ms. C., "Oh, you sit down and let me get that coffee for you."

We had reason to suspect that Madame Butterfly would end our little party, because she had a reputation of being a strict and unfeeling woman. We knew she was aware of all the games inmates played. Therefore, we all joined together to sabotage any attempts to have Madame Butterfly transferred to our department.

One by one, we would stop by Mr. S.'s desk and try to con him into halting Madame Butterfly's transfer. I would bring him coffee and donuts, and quietly suggest, "Boy, it sure is nice and quiet around here. I hope we don't get an officer who stirs things up." Another inmate, Wanda P., would follow me and drop a hint or two with something like, "I sure hope we don't get one of those hard-nosed officers who is always jumping on inmates."

Each time we offered him a bribe. Something sweet. His diet didn't allow it, but we were desparate and he loved sweets. But he would just take our gracious offerings and point to the door because he knew what we were up to.

Our under-the-table efforts were all in vain; Madame Butterfly joined our department. To this day I'm ashamed of the way I acted, because within a very short time we all realized no one was going to lose weight because of Madame Butterfly's presence in the office. Not only did she look the other way whenever we raided the goodie table, she proved to be one of the most sincere and caring ladies on the prison staff.

My newfound respect and appreciation for certain gray suits and staff members continued to grow as I ever so slowly began to realize that not all T.D.C. employees viewed inmates as animals.

Yet I'm forced to admit there have been times when I saw them that way. My first encounter with the base lust of some of the humans with whom I was forced to live might be considered comical now, but at the time they shocked me.

Let me explain.

The Mountain View Unit was originally a home for male juvenile delinquents. It is said that the incarcerated boys were treated abusively and many either died or were accidentally killed. Their little bodies, when unclaimed by family, were supposedly buried on the prison property in a cemetery known as Boot Hill. When the juvenile facility was shut down, some of the employees who worked for the Youth Correctional Center stayed on to join the staff of the women's prison, and from them many stories and legends were passed on to explain some of the strange things that happened within our prison walls.

Throughout the entire prison, but especially in the dorm located nearest Boot Hill, there are regular reports of strange happenings and unexplainable occurrences. Inmates often report hearing children's voices and cries during the night. Many an inmate has been awakened in the middle of the night by the "touch" of an unseen spirit. Blankets are jerked off while they sleep. Toilets flush when no one is near. Kitchen workers hear knocking sounds and whimpers or cries coming from the vaults where supplies are stored.

Gray suits and staff members are not immune to these strange manifestations either. Once, in the kitchen, an officer was checking to insure that all the doors leading to the outside docks were locked. As she turned to leave, all the doors flew open. She ran screaming from the kitchen and refused to return to that area alone.

Having heard all these stories when I arrived at Mountain View, I laughed them off. But one afternoon, while watching a football game on television, I decided I wanted a snack, so I walked back to my room at half-time to get one. As I was passing through the deserted dorm hall, I noticed a bed in an unoccupied room literally jumping off the floor. Suddenly I believed! The little ghosts had invaded our dorm!

I ran back to the dayroom to tell someone. Everyone looked at me in astonishment when I told them what was happening, but Rosalinda just laughed. "Baby, them ain't no baby ghosts. That's two bitches makin' love down there."

In the years that followed, I would see women "getting it on" under the bleachers, "making out" in the gym and "lovin' it up" in the rec yard under the moon. Some women get so hungry and thirsty for each other that they'll get together in the bathroom. Before it became policy for an officer to be posted in the dorms, I used to see two women making love to each other in the dayroom, in plain view of everyone in the dorm. They completely ignored the rest of us. They just didn't care.

A lot of violence erupts because of these relationships.

Vicious battles most often break out between bickering couples, between stud broads when one makes a "hit" or a move on the other's lover, and between a stud broad sticking up for her lover and a straight.

For example, a big fight occurred one day in E dorm between Doberman, a heavy-set white girl who looked like a male wrestler, and Pit Bull, a stocky, hateful black woman. The fight began when Pit Bull got into an argument with Doberman's "wife" (her homosexual lover). Doberman stepped in to protect her lover and E Dorm turned into a battleground. Pit Bull, however, was too much for the white girl and whipped her good. Not satisfied with just whipping her, she broke a glass and threatened to cut Doberman's throat. Finally, the guard realized something was going on inside the dorm and rushed in. Both inmates were restrained and removed from the dorm for disciplinary action. However, since E Dorm was the home of the warden's girls, the two women received only a slap on the wrist and instructions to kiss and make up.

For the most part, when lesbians fight the action is confined to the individuals, though occasionally a fight between them can quickly spread and involve everyone. I once got caught up in one myself. About sixty-five inmates had turned out for the rec yard and a fight broke out between two lovers. An officer, a young new mother who had just returned to duty from maternity leave, tried to break up the fight and suddenly found herself being attacked by others. A few of us saw what was happening and rushed in to pull her out of the fight. In the process, someone slapped me.

I forgot all about the young officer and jumped for the bitch who slapped me. Before I could grab her, someone lifted me off the ground and held me up with my legs dangling in the air. I looked around and saw it was a tall, dark stud broad. She kept me from getting involved in the fight until other officers arrived. As I look back, it's a good thing she did because there is no telling what I would have done to someone who had the gall to slap me.

One especially difficult issue in the art of survival in prison has to do with sex. How does a normal, healthy woman behind bars handle her desires? If you're not homosexual and you don't want to mess around with the male guards, the answer is simple: It's a living hell!

I had always taken pride in being a strong woman. "You can do anything you want to do," I would tell myself when times got rough. So when I first entered T.D.C. I made up my mind that sex simply would not be a part of my life until I was released. I resolved to put my mind on other things.

Easier said than done.

If you are someone who eats a lot of sweets and overnight you are cut off from all sweets, naturally your body goes through withdrawal. You become moody and irritable. Everything and everyone gets on your nerves. I'm a living witness that you go through these changes (and many more) when you are cut off from sex.

I found myself avoiding conversations with other inmates when the subject of sex came up. I even avoided watching any television program that had sexual allusions, and stuck to sports or the news. I didn't watch stories about men and women for fear that once the lights went out I would end up dreaming about something I couldn't have. Many nights I dreamt about it anyway. I would wake up in a cold sweat with my heart racing. When I sat up, looked around, and realized where I was, the tears would begin to fall. The harder I tried not to cry, the more I did because the dreams were so real.

It was the same dream over and over again. I was in bed with a man I loved. I could actually feel what was happening to me. I knew it was real, because how else can you explain waking up with a pounding heart and a shortness of breath, and a pulsating, tingling, sensation that comes only from sex? Yet, of course it couldn't be. It was absolute frustration! Just another reminder of what I had been forced to give up for *nothing*. The dreams rekindled my hatred—not so much for anyone in particular anymore, but for the justice system that was so blind to me.

Other inmates found their own ways of dealing with the problem.

The first time I ever heard anyone talk about "Henry" I couldn't figure out who he was. Two inmates would be talking in the dorm and one of them would say, "Child, I need to go see Henry." Or I'd see a girl go to the shower and when it became obvious she was spending more time in there than allowed, someone would yell out, "Damn, Henry must be good tonight. I better go see him myself."

Who the hell was Henry?

Then I found out. A few of the inmates had tampered with one of the showers until they had it fixed where it would shoot out a concentrated stream of water. By allowing the water to strike their body near the clitoris, they could achieve an orgasm. That shower was Henry.

An "uninitiated" inmate named Hilda was once taking a shower when the inmate showering next to her began to shake and moan. Scared to death, Hilda asked, "Honey, you all right? Are you sick?"

The inmate just continued to shake and groan and then she sort of fell backwards, knocking Hilda over. She was ready to call for a guard, but then the inmate explained, "I was visiting Henry and it was so good I just lost my balance."

I never thought of myself as naive, but the way these girls talked about masturbation, I couldn't believe it. One day they were sitting there giggling, laughing, and carrying on so much that I asked, "What's so funny?"

One of the ladies answered, "Daisy said she makes love to her boyfriend every day."

"What are you talking, Daisy?"

Daisy answered, "My boyfriend. My deodorant. You get yourself one of those roll-on deodorant sticks, the kind with the ball on the top, wrap it in a washrag or sock, go into the bathroom, and get on your thing and you'll think you got a man in there."

One of the girls laughed, "Daisy, you got to be one sick woman!"

"I'm not sick. I got to do something. Shit. I'm not sick. Y'all the ones that are sick. If I didn't get it off, I'd go crazy!"

Others evidently felt the same way, because one night I was trying to go to sleep when I heard something strange from the cubicle across the way. Angel, a very hefty inmate, was moaning, "Shit, shit, oh, shit-shit-shit." I sat up to see what was the matter and saw her lying on her bed, masturbating. Real loudly I said, "Damn, there's no privacy anywhere around here." I figured that when she realized there was an eyewitness to what was going on, she would display some discretion. No, she just kept it up until she was finished.

The next day, I was in my cubicle, playing possum, and I heard her talking to her friends.

"Ooooooowee, I was thinking about Rayford last night and I was thinking he was making love to me and it sure was good. And I just had to have it. And I got it, but old nosey over there kept saying, 'Damn, you can't get no privacy around here.' I sure hated for her to see it, but it ain't my fault that she sleeps all day and stays up all night. If she had been asleep, she'd never have known what was going on. And I had to have it, so I got it while she went back to sleep."

I spoke from my bed, "No, I didn't go to sleep. I heard you last night."

Angel laughed, "Well, I'm sorry. I didn't mean for you to hear me, but you should have been asleep. You ought to be like normal people. Normal people sleep at night and are up during the day. You ain't normal, Joyce."

I didn't accept that for one minute. I knew who was normal and who wasn't, and I knew who had to get out of there while she was still normal.

6

Fresh Meat, Stud Broads, and Pipeline Lovers

I was seventeen years old when I met Miss Joyce. I had just entered T.D.C. on a murder charge and my attitude was a total disaster. I immediately got into several fights. I was so bad I was moved to a different dorm, and when I walked in I said, "I'm doing ninety-nine years and I don't want to be fucked with."

It didn't take me long to recognize the fact that Miss Joyce was something special. Everyone called her Mother, or Auntie, or Sis; and those who didn't use these family names called her Miss Joyce.

The first time I ever talked to Miss Joyce, we were in the shower. She looked at me and asked, "How old are you, child?"

I snapped off an answer: "Seventeen, if it's any of your business."

She just shook her head, and I remember this sad look in her eyes as she said, "I have a daughter your age, and I can see right now if you don't change your attitude, I'm going to change it for you."

I'll say this: She did change my attitude. In fact, Miss Joyce, or Mama, as I learned to call her, changed my life. She taught me how to talk and walk, how to eat at the dining hall table like a lady, and most of all, she taught me how to love and respect God, myself, and others.

It all started when I stole a pair of headphones from another inmate. When it was discovered that I had stolen them, Mama made me return the headphones to the lady and apologize. I thought the incident was closed but that night, after lights out, while I was in my bed, Mama came to my cubicle and told me to follow her. We went to her cubicle and she told me to get down on my knees. I thought we were going to pray. I never even saw the extension cord. I remember her saying, "You are not going to do any more stealing in here."

Then she whipped my butt and sent me back to bed. I never stole nothing else again.

–Shawana Sims
Mountain View Inmate

Shawana was one of the many granddaughters I acquired in prison. She had never enjoyed a parental relationship in her life, so I guess I became the mother she never really had. After I spanked her little bottom for stealing, she grabbed me around the legs, crying, and promised she would never steal anything again as long as she lived. I really think she was grateful to find someone that cared enough for her to make her behave like a normal child.

I found myself caring not only for Shawana, but for the other children who were finding their way to prison. I began to find myself in the position of being the mother hen for all the babies who needed my love, strength, protection, and guidance. Looking back, I realize that those inmate children provided me an opportunity to become a surrogate mother—the parent I couldn't be to my own children. In a sense, I needed them more than they needed me.

When I first went into prison, women under twenty-one made up less than two percent of the prison population. Today that figure has shot up to almost ten percent. It used to break my heart, watching the dorms fill up with more and more young girls arrested for writing hot checks or possession of dope, and then thrown in with hardened criminals.

They're called "new meat" or "fresh meat," and they're just sixteen or seventeen years old. When they first come in, they think they're tough. For months, they've been laying up in a county jail where someone has told them how to act when they get to prison, but nothing can really prepare them. They arrive, innocent as little lambs, and the vultures descend. Stud broads abuse them and Cell Block bitches bully them. Scared, they move under the wing of an older woman. If they are lucky, the adopted guardian guides them in the right direc-tion. If they aren't, they proceed to get a cram course in how to become a habitual criminal.

Old-timers can put a con job on the new meat like you wouldn't believe. No sooner does a youngster walk through the door when an older one slides over and opens up a conversation. "Oh, ain't she a pretty thing. She reminds me of my daughter."

Then she'll proceed to help the new meat get settled in. While helping the child make her bed and arrange her belongings in her new house, the seasoned inmate will carry on what seems to be just small talk. She'll ask questions about the youngster's crime and sentence; but mostly her interest is centered around the new arrival's family. Are they working? Will they be sending the girl money? She'll feed her goodies and offer the use of makeup or other personal things until the girl's first visit to the commissary. Everything is geared to winning her affection and trust.

First they'll con the new meat into cleaning up their house once a week; then they'll con her into doing their washing.

"Honey, what you doing today?"

The new girl might answer, "Nothing."

"Honey," the old timer pleads, "wash this for Mama today. I'm not feeling too well."

Before the new girl knows it, washing Mama's things becomes a regular weekly ritual.

When the new meat's money begins coming in, the old-timer sits right down with her and explains how the commissary works. She'll help her new daughter fill out the commissary list and you can safely assume that many of the items purchased will be for Mama's benefit.

Eventually, Mama might say one day, "I've got me a package to pick up over in F Dorm, but I've got to be somewhere else today and I can't get over there."

Anytime the word "package" is used, it means contraband or illegal merchandise that someone has obtained for another inmate. The package might be anything from sugar and food out of the dining hall to drugs. Anyone caught transporting contraband automatically receives a case, so anytime an old-timer can con someone else into picking up a package, she will.

"We sure do need that package. But I can't get over there to pick it up."

The daughter, anxious to please and show appreciation for all the old-timer has done for her, will volunteer, "Don't you worry about that package. I'll pick it up for you."

Another common convenience that old-timers use new girls for is protection. Let's say the old-timer gets into a fight with someone. She'll say a few words and then the youngster, who doesn't want someone jumping on her Mama, will get into the action. When this happens, Mama kind of slides into the background, and when the law finally gets involved, the daughter is doing all the yelling, screaming, cursing and maybe even kicking and punching. Guess who gets the case for disturbance or fighting? Mama will be very sympathetic over her daughter's case.

Sometimes two old-timers work together to rope in some new meat. One old-timer will immediately get friendly with a new arrival. After a day or two, the second finds an excuse to pick on the newcomer. She will accuse her of some supposed affront, like going into her cubicle without permission. "I'll tell you right now, little bitch," she'll threaten, "if it ever happens again I'm going to kick your everlovin' ass all over this dorm!"

Now the first old-timer jumps in. "There ain't going to be no ass-kicking because this little girl is like my daughter!" She'll play the role of the protector to the hilt. "You mess with this girl, and

you're messin' with me, and you don't want none of me 'cause I'll
flat tear your fuckin' ass up."

The "confrontation" is avoided, the scared newcomer is grateful,
and the first old-timer has established her position. To top it off,
several days later the second one manages to come around and play
the part of an apologetic woman. Before you know it, all three are
big buddies and sharing everything—mostly the newcomer's things.

The stud broads, of course, look over every new arrival with more
than passing curiosity.

Unlike in male prisons, newcomers to T.D.C. units are not raped
or forced into homosexuality by other inmates. Participants get into
the game willingly. It probably has something to with the fact that if
they come into prison accustomed to being a follower, they simply
continue to follow the leader. Some, I'm convinced, come in starved
for affection. When a stud broad showers them with something
they've never had, they willingly succumb to her advances.

Others merely recognize the advantages of playing the homosexual
game. I've seen several stud broads with as many as five or six "stable
sisters" (or "wives") who contribute heavily to the stud broad's
welfare. Each inmate is allowed to spend sixty dollars every two
weeks in the commissary, and it's a common sight to see a stud broad
making "his" rounds regularly, instructing each stable sister on how
to make out her commissary order. It's not unusual for the "wife" to
spend as much as forty, fifty, even sixty dollars on her "husband." A
stud broad with several wives taking care of "him" is indeed living
high on the hog, while his wives have to spend every day hustling or
boosting necessities from fellow inmates.

If an inmate is homosexual when she arrives, chances are that she
will immediately fall in with the homosexual community inside. If
she starts out straight, she may or may not become homosexual; it
just depends on the type of individual she is. One thing I have learned,
though—straights who come in and participate in the homosexual
game go back to the free world as straights, not homosexuals. They
might play the game for a while, but as soon as they hit that door
they're ready for a man again.

Other straights laugh about this game of homosexuality. They even
write poems and jokes about it. This rap song, written by an inmate,

pretty well sums up the feelings held by straights for gays—especially stud broads:

> *I wanna tell you about a certain lady*
> *Her style is really slick and her actions really shady.*
> *I don't like the way she carries herself,*
> *Taking people so fast til' there ain't nothing left.*
> *She's a stud broad!*
>
> *She wears dark shades; she walks real hard,*
> *To give you an answer, she gives you a nod.*
> *She thinks she's fantastic and has finesse,*
> *Thinkin' she's a man with big titties on her chest.*
> *She's a stud broad!*
>
> *She walks around, holdin' her crotch,*
> *Feeling for something that she ain't got,*
> *When all the while she uses her tongue,*
> *Lickin' and suckin' until you cum.*
> *She's a stud broad!*
>
> *Today is commissary and she's on her way,*
> *To meet the little lady with the bag for pay,*
> *When she looks in the bag and sees it all ain't there,*
> *She grabs her by the throat and drags her by the hair.*
> *She's a stud broad!*
>
> *Well the time is right, she schemes and figures,*
> *So she goes to the dayroom to get her a jigger.*
> *Her and her people go under the bed*
> *She gets a little sugar and she gives a little head.*
> *She's a stud broad!*
>
> *While they're under the bed, getting it on,*
> *The police in the pipe chase gets on the phone.*
> *They get caught in the act, stark naked in fact.*
> *Do you know what the law throw up in their face?*
> *Yes, that's right—the Big Sex Case.*
> *She's a stud broad!*
>
> *Well, the lady comes up and makes parole,*
> *So the prison game started getting old.*
> *So she puts on make-up, throws on a skirt,*
> *She's going to the free world, and she's ready to flirt.*
> *But she's a stud broad!*

Stud broads will come into prison talking hard, walking with their shoulders squared, slouched over, and acting just like a man. When they walk, they're always holding onto or scratching their crotch, and it's impossible not to laugh because they haven't got a thing to scratch or hold onto.

What's really comical is when they get their monthly period. All month they've been walking around portraying the big tough guy and then that time of the month arrives. All of a sudden, they're walking around with cramps, or lying in their bed moaning, going through menstrual pains.

Or on Mother's Day, when their mothers come to the prison for a visit. All of a sudden they appear in a dress, high heels, stockings, makeup, and feminine hairdos. To us, they looked like the female impersonators who walk the streets of the free world. For three hundred and sixty-four days a year they've been going around picking fights and bullying their wives, and then that one day they're suddenly dainty, delicate vessels of femininity.

I should point out that not all prison homosexuals conduct their preferred lifestyle in a flagrant manner. Some are so inconspicuous that you would never guess they were lesbian. Neither should it be assumed that the pursuit of sexual pleasure at any cost is restricted to prison inmates. Some officers, male and female, are just as obsessive.

We called him Bull. He was a huge white hulk of a man who was in charge of the kitchen. We heard how he had his own thing going with several of the inmates working under him—literally working under him. The things that went on between Bull and his "heifers" (as we called them) were well known to us inmates; officers, who must have also known about them, seemed to simply turn their heads the other way. It appeared that nothing would ever be done about Bull's sexcapades.

These were restricted to anal or oral sex because Bull didn't want to get any of his heifers pregnant and end up with a young calf. His main heifer, Patti Ann, was a very small white woman who barely weighed one hundred pounds. Not only did she keep Bull satisfied, but she was also able to become the true manager of that kitchen. In fact, it was referred to as "Patti Ann's kitchen" by the inmates. If anyone needed a day off, a better job, or a favor, Patti Ann was the one to see. She held this position of power because whenever Bull wanted sex, she made herself available. That kitchen storeroom door was closed to prying eyes many times each week as Bull and his heifer conducted "inventory" inside.

Eventually, the complaints and reports must have become too numerous to ignore, because the authorities, instead of disciplining Bull, transferred Patti Ann into the yard, leaving Bull free to pursue his sexual pleasures elsewhere.

However, Bull and one of his heifers made what was to be a costly mistake. They forced a newly arrived nineteen-year-old white girl to perform oral sex on him. The newcomer, an inexperienced and unwilling participant, was threatened into satisfying Bull's lust, but in the course of the act, she gagged and Bull ejaculated all over her blouse. The poor girl went into hysterics and was rushed to the unit infirmary, where the doctor calmed her down and verified that male semen was present on her clothes. The unit warden attempted to contain the incident, but it quickly became the talk of every inmate and officer in the prison. An investigation was conducted and, although Bull was guilty of rape, he was merely transferred to a male unit while his young victim was admitted to psychotherapy.

Just as sexual misconduct is not limited to inmates, neither is homosexuality. Let me tell you what we heard about "Love Child." She was an officer who, it was rumored, was also a lesbian and a drug peddler. Peggy Sue, a white stud broad inmate who recognized a golden opportunity when she saw one, "fell in love" with Love Child. Peggy Sue used to say, "If the Love Child wants to play, she'll have to pay."

And pay she did—in free dope. The affair went on for quite a while, but as usually happens, the stud broad and the hippie had a big lover's quarrel. Peggy Sue, realizing that she was about to lose out to another woman, decided that if she couldn't have the Love Child and her drugs, no one else would. She went to the law and told them everything.

Peggy Sue cut a deal where she wouldn't get a case in exchange for setting Love Child up for a bust. Word had it that the authorities had Peggy Sue order some dope. Love Child promised to bring some to work with her the next day. When she came in, prison police were waiting at the front gate. Love Child was shaken down like a common inmate and busted for bringing in pills and marijuana. She was not allowed inside the prison that day and we never saw her again.

It's also necessary to point out that even though there are so many homosexual relationships in prison, many don't necessarily involve sex. It can actually be nothing more than a proprietary or companionable relationship. A stud broad might have "wives" in other dorms and only occasionally have an opportunity to see them in places like the dining hall, rec yard or school. The relationship might involve only a stolen kiss or a little hand-holding when a guard isn't looking. Of course, when sex is the goal, lovers will manage to get together even if they live in separate dorms.

One of my children, whom I now refer to as Bonehead because she acted so stupidly, came into prison a scared, naive child. I took her under my wing; but after a while she sort of drifted into areas I didn't approve of. She began playing the homosexual game.

One evening, Bonehead and Conchita signed out for the writ room. As soon as they signed in, they checked out again. One of the guards became suspicious over their brief stay, and when she called the dorm to see if they had returned, she discovered they had disappeared. A search was immediately begun, but still the two girls could not be found. More officers got involved. While checking a small room inside the chapel, one officer had trouble opening the door. When he finally managed to push it open, there was Bonehead, buck naked on the floor with her stud broad Conchita.

I lost all respect for the girl and ceased to treat her as one of my own. Soon she came to me and wanted to talk, but I pushed her away. "I don't want you even talking to me, girl. I just want you to get out of my face."

She was pretty upset about my attitude, but my patience had been worn out. "You prove to me that you've changed. Maybe then we can talk."

It wasn't just her stupid homosexual date that had upset me. By now I had simply turned my head to homosexual antics and adopted the attitude, *to each his own*. Some of my best friends in prison were gay and we had strong, healthy friendships. I never held their sexual preference against them. But Bonehead's case was different.

She had so much potential. She was, without question, one of the smartest inmates in prison. She was a girl who never cracked a book but still made straight A's in the prison classes. She was also very good-looking and had a great personality. And with all these gifts, she was constantly getting into trouble and receiving cases from the law. Her problem was that she got herself into prison as a result of being a follower—she allowed people to lead her. She had followed someone on a robbery and was caught. Once inside prison, she continued to be a follower. Despite my efforts to help her think and act for herself, she chose to follow stud broads and others who were only interested in what they could get out of her. I simply had no patience with that sort of spinelessness.

New arrivals not only have to be on the alert for old-timers, stud broads, and lecherous "gray suits," but they also have to watch out for "Cell Block bitches."

They're called this because they live in what is known as the Cell Block, a cinder block building in which the troublemakers and incorrigibles—those who have received major cases for sexual misconduct or fighting with a weapon—are housed. Many of the inmates living in the Cell Block are indeed bitches and are adept at getting not only themselves in trouble, but others as well.

In my job at the Education & Recreation building, I often had to travel throughout the prison to deliver vocational and college course schedules. Without exception, the Cell Block was always the noisiest place in the entire complex. Inside, the inmates screamed and cursed at each other, radios blared from each cell, and the volume on the lone television set was wide open all day long.

Being moved to the Cell Block is supposed to be a form of punishment, but no one ever convinced me of that. To begin with, the inmates there enjoy the same privileges as those in population. They are allowed to go to the commissary, school, rec yard, writ room, dining hall, or anywhere else. In regular dorms, as many as thirty-four women are crammed together, but in the Cell Block, inmates actually have more room because they are housed in cells which hold only one or two inmates. Also, in that these are lock-down cells, inmates can request that their cell be locked if they don't wish to be disturbed. In this manner, an inmate can enjoy private time for sleeping, reading, relaxing, or whatever, without being interrupted by another inmate.

Another advantage to living in Cell Block is being able to keep your own clothes inside your cell. Each inmate in a dorm is allowed to keep only socks, slips, and underwear in her house. Everything else is stored in the clothing room, which is located in a building outside the dorms. Every day, rain or shine, cold or hot, we'd have to leave the dorm, go to the clothing room, and be issued pajamas or a night gown, clothes, and a towel for the next day. The only time a dorm inmate can get more than one day's issue is on Friday, when she is allowed to pull three sets—for Saturday, Sunday and Monday. At the end of each day, dirty clothes are turned into the officer on duty and sent to the laundry. Get caught with more than one set of work clothes or one towel or one pair of pajamas—except on weekends—and you could get a case. Too many cases and it's off to the Cell Block, where you can have all the clothes you want.

True, a stint in the Cell Block results in a loss of good time, which in turn means a longer prison sentence, but anyone serving an aggravated ninety-nine or life sentence doesn't worry too much about losing good time. They don't get too upset when threatened by an officer or guard with a case. "Put your pen in the wind," an inmate will say, indicating that she is doing so much time she doesn't care whether she gets a case or not. In fact, many inmates will deliberately catch a case just to get sent to the Cell Block so they can join a lover or a friend, or simply because they enjoy living in the Cell Block more than in the dorms. The same holds true for some Cell Block inmates who like their quarters so much that they will continue to break rules in order to stay.

The women in the Cell Block are actually babied by the administration. The attitude is, "Let them do what they want as long as they don't get too far out of line." In other words, normal rules and regulations are not enforced in the Cell Block because the officers are encouraged to overlook infractions. The unwritten policy: don't get them stirred up.

Since these inmates don't really care about losing good time and have a license to act off, they are in a perfect position to intimidate new meat. Remember my granddaughter Shawana? When she first entered prison she had an altercation with an inmate named Booger. Booger was the notorious troublemaker who had spent most of her prison time in Cell Block. One day she decided she would whip up on some new meat. Shawana, although a tiny thing, is a tough little sister. She slipped a padlock into a sock and when Booger came at her, she let the troublemaker find out what trouble was. Fortunately, other inmates stopped the fight before there was any serious injury.

"I'll get you one day," Booger said.

Once you make an enemy in prison, you're never safe. Even if you are moved to a different dorm or placed in protective custody you're not safe, because sooner or later that enemy will catch you alone and when she does, she'll attack. You might be returning to your dorm one day and knock on the door to be admitted. While you are waiting for the guard, your enemy comes around the corner, sees you, and immediately starts a fight. The guard sees the fight but can't step in to stop it. You'll first have to call for help, then wait for that help to arrive. Meanwhile, you're in a fight with your enemy, perhaps with her friends, too.

When the fight is finally stopped, everyone gets a case. Again, it doesn't matter that you were defending yourself. Prison officials take the attitude that you should have run for help or not fought back. Yet if you walk away or stand there and take someone's abuse, you lose the respect of the other inmates and then they'll start walking all over you.

This is a difficult position to be in, and one that Shawanna was faced with. Several years after she had bested Booger, she found herself alone one day with the troublemaker, who immediately started a fight. For once, Shawana used her head. She was in the process of appealing her case in an attempt to get her ninety-nine-year sentence reduced and was determined to avoid trouble at all costs—even at the risk of losing some inmates' respect or even her own self-respect. She refused to fight Booger but promised her, "I'm not going to mess with you now, but if I don't get my time reduced, I'm coming back to whip your ass, Booger. You can count on it."

Shawana got whipped up on that day, but she got the best of Booger. She received a reduction in her sentence, and will soon be eligible for parole.

Cell Block bitches will even pick on old-timers living in minimum custody dorms who are trying to do their time quietly. My friend Gee Gee was once returning to her dorm from the commissary when she was approached by one of the Cell Block inmates.

"Give me one of your soft drinks, bitch," the woman said in a loud, threatening voice.

Gee Gee just looked at her for a moment and finally said, "I don't think so."

"If you don't give me one, I'll just take it. Don't you know I live in the Cell Block?"

Gee Gee set her bag down and answered, "If you think you're going to take it, you just come right on because I'm going to give it to you, but not the way you want it."

The Cell Block inmate backed off, but if Gee Gee had not been the strong person she is, she would have given up the soda. The surprising point to this illustration is that the Cell Block inmate backed away, because if she had really wanted the soda, she would have attacked Gee Gee without fear of reprisal. Gee Gee, however, would have received a case and a loss of good time. In prison, you're damned if you do and damned if you don't.

Not everyone sent to the Cell Block is a hard case or a trouble-maker. Take Money Signs. Money Signs is a tall, dark-skinned beauty with long legs and long hair. She has a way with people and I don't think there is anyone in prison that doesn't like her. She is outgoing, fun-loving, and so well liked that she is spoiled. Everyone waits on her hand and foot. But Money Signs is the unit joker—always talking, always stirring things up. Nothing destructive, and certainly nothing cruel or vicious. She's just full of mischief, a trait which has won her the prison record for most cases received for rules infractions.

She is the only woman in prison to ever have received a case for beating up a trash container. What happened could happen only to Money Signs.

Inmates walking outside a dorm are not allowed to stop and carry on a conversation with an inmate inside the dorm. But the windows provide a lot of temptation. If an inmate is standing near the window, sees a friend passing by on the outside, and just yells "hello!" to her, she will receive a case. One day an officer saw an animated Money Signs standing in front of a dorm window clowning, laughing and apparently talking to someone on the inside. However, she couldn't see the person Money Signs was talking to, so she couldn't write her up (for this offense, two names have to be on the case). Knowing Money Signs as I do, it is highly possible that there was no one inside the window; she was simply acting out a charade to bait the officer. But she carried the bit too far. In her clowning around, she accidentally kicked a trash can and the officer, unable to write her up for carrying on a conversation, immediately wrote her up for "Whipping a trash can."

On another occasion an officer walked onto the rec yard and saw her standing in the bleachers giving an impromptu concert—a Gladys Knight imitation—to an empty field. Her case: "Being out of place."

She once received a case for "Bowling in the dorm." Her bowling ball was an empty five-gallon peanut butter can and her pins were the inmates (and officers) walking down the dorm aisle.

If it is possible to get a case for breaking every petty rule within a prison, Money Signs has done it. Including the one for "Eating the evidence."

One morning, as was her daily routine, she swept by the dining hall for breakfast. She did not go in; she never had to. Inmates working in the dining hall kept their eye out for Money Signs. As she passed by, someone would shoot her a breakfast package. She would grab it and eat her breakfast as she walked to class or to work.

On this particular morning, however, an officer saw her accept the package and immediately yelled out, "Hey you!"

Money Signs knew she was in trouble, so she started running.

And she runs like a deer. Anyone else would have run up the hallway and tried to hide, but Money Signs ran right through the officer-filled Count Office with an officer hot on her trail.

She was too fast for him and lost him by slipping through the officer's exit, walking around the building, and entering the front door as if nothing had happened.

And as she ran, she was quickly eating her breakfast. If she was caught they would confiscate the package, take a picture of it as evidence, and give her a case. Knowing she would not only lose the food but receive a case, she was determined to at least have the enjoyment of finishing her meal. When they finally caught up with her, she was walking sedately, empty-handed. Without it they couldn't give her a case for possessing contraband. But they gave her one—for "eating the evidence"—anyway.

Just as Money Signs was the joker of the unit, Denise was the loud-mouth. Denise was built like Tarzan's chimp, Cheetah. She was bow-legged, pigeon-toed, short, and black, and had the dirtiest mouth in prison. She talked so much and so loudly that when the law saw her coming, they turned their backs and ignored her. Whenever she walked into a room, there was no doubt in anyone's mind that Denise had arrived.

"What's this mother-fuckin' shit here? I ain't going to eat this goddamned shit!" And she would waddle up to the guard in charge, cursing every step of the way. Instead of reprimanding her, the guard would actually try to ignore her. She was perhaps the only inmate that could intimidate the guards and officers, and she did it with her mouth. She would come walking into the Count Office and that mouth of hers would be running. "Come on, bring your mother-fuckin' asses on right now and talk to me now because I ain't going to be standing up here for all this mother-fuckin' bullshit! Y'all know that bitch is wrong for writing me up with that bullshit."

The officers would turn around and might say, "Denise, control your mouth or you're going to get another case."

"Ok, ok, ok, ok," she would say, and then turn to me and in her loudest voice ask, "Joyce, why are these mother-fuckers fuckin' with me like this?"

Inmates loved her. She was foul-mouthed, but she was one of the funniest women in prison and kept everyone laughing from daylight to dark. It was almost impossible to play any games with Denise, because her mouth would keep running and everyone would be laughing too hard to concentrate on the game. "Hey, bitch!" she might yell out to one particularly well-endowed inmate during a volleyball game, "You better not get too close to this net because I might think those big titties are the volleyball and smash you across the net."

Sometimes she would dance for us and the strangest thing would happen. She would do a split on the ground and her little legs would be just as straight pool cues, not bowed a bit.

However, a couple of years ago, Denise was removed from population and, at her request, placed in isolation. She had been diagnosed with AIDS.

If there is one policy within the prison that both scares and infuriates the inmates and creates an underlying sense of apprehension, it's the prison policy on AIDS.

Prison officials tried to educate us about AIDS. A video was produced and aired over the television system which explained the disease and told us what we should and shouldn't do. What they didn't tell us was who among us had AIDS.

"See that girl over there?" Carol asked me one day while we were sitting in the dayroom.

"Did you know that she has AIDS? That's why she's been going back and forth to the hospital. I'm mad at these bastards. That girl has been living next to me all this time, sneezing, coughing. I've been over there trying to help and comfort her, and she's had AIDS the whole time. What if she got a cut or hurt herself and I contracted it just for taking care of her?"

Therein lies the problem. If an inmate has AIDS, not only are fellow inmates not informed, but the infected inmate is not removed from population unless she requests it. What upsets the majority of us is the fact that acts of violence between inmates are so common. You run the risk of exposure if you follow your instinct to go help whoever is left bleeding and hurt. Should inmates then stop helping each other?

Living with someone who has AIDS and not knowing it can up your risk of contracting the disease. But if a victim's secret does get out, other inmates can really get on her case, which can't be too good for the her emotional state. "Bitch, I'm not going to argue with your AIDS-carryin' ass. You'll never get a chance to bite me and give me your dirty disease."

An inmate will be isolated from population if she requests it, but it isn't really isolation. She is provided her own cell in Segregation, but she doesn't lose any of her privileges. She is still allowed to go to chow, visit the commissary, go to school, and walk and mingle with population.

There are a number of ladies whom I know to have AIDS. A few moved to Segregation but most continue to live in population. It's a controversial subject that seems doomed to boil over one of these days.

One of my associates at work had AIDS. She had been in prison for four years before she found out. To illustrate how fast the prison grapevine works, she was called to report to the infirmary for her test results. Before she could walk from the E&R building to the medical office, someone had already called and told me they had heard from someone else that the woman had AIDS. The prison population knew the test results before the poor woman herself did. No one had the nerve to tell her as she walked by because she had a reputation of going off, so she didn't learn her condition—even though we all knew—until she arrived at the infirmary.

Naturally, she was upset about her condition, but even more upsetting was the fact that the officials were less concerned about her than they were over the possibility that she might have contracted the disease from a guard. They grilled her for a long time, trying to find out which guards she had had sex with. Finally, they accepted her denial of any prison sexual activities and concluded that she must have arrived in prison with the disease four years earlier.

She was a sweet girl, but she was illiterate. She liked me because I would read her letters to her. Someone else would write letters that she would dictate—in exchange for payment of some item from the commissary—but she always brought me her letters to read to her. Most of them came from male prisoners within the Texas prison system.

Prison pen pals are common among the inmates. We had what they call the "Dear Abby" column in the prison newspaper, *The Echo*, where men and women put their names in the column asking for someone to write them a letter. There is never any shortage of letters. The men even go a little further. If a woman's name is mentioned in a newspaper article, she can expect up to a dozen letters from male prisoners.

And before you know it, a long distance love affair is born. There are some women in prison who have been carrying on such love affairs for years, professing their love daily to men they've never laid eyes on. Inmates are so starved for affection and attention that these love affairs by proxy go on and on. They'll write each other for years until one of them is released; and after that, they'll never correspond again.

However, I know of one instance where the couple actually did get married. The affair had begun in the Dallas county jail through what is known as the underground phone system. In the county jail, inmates are able to flush all the water out of the toilet pipes by continuous flushing. Once the pipes are empty, they make perfect telephone lines. You can lean into the toilet and talk to people in the tanks below or above you through the empty pipes. Cora spent quite a bit of time in the Dallas county jail before being transferred to Mountain View. While there she fell in love with James, a sexy-voiced male inmate whom she talked to daily, sometimes hourly, over the jail pipeline.

At that time, inmates could get married by proxy. The jail chaplain would go to the women's tank and say the wedding vows with the bride, then visit the men's tank, where he would have the groom repeat the vows. For a few dollars, you were then married, complete with license and wedding certificate. This is exactly what Cora did—she married her pipeline lover.

After being sent to separate state prisons the two continued to correspond by mail. James was released early and made arrangements to visit the wife he had never seen. She had his name put on the visitor's list and awaited his visit with all the nervous excitement of a new bride.

The big day arrived and Cora strode into the visitor's room where two men were sitting. She immediately scoped the two out. One was handsome, well-dressed, and smiling. The other was the foulest man she had ever seen—coarse, unkempt, and just down-right ugly. Cora never hesitated and walked directly up to Mr. Charming, seated herself, and began to talk to him.

Then she felt a hand on her shoulder and turning around, saw another inmate glaring down at her. "You're talking to my visitor," she announced. "That other dude is yours." Cora smiled sheepishly, stood up, walked over to Mr. Ugly and asked, "Are you James?"

He smiled through some ugly teeth and nodded his head.

She smiled at him, turned around, walked out and never looked back. "That was the first and last time I saw him," she told us.

She never wrote him again, and when she finally got out, it's my understanding that she didn't even try to locate him. She just filed for divorce and went on her way.

7

A Call To Dallas

If Joyce has a fault, it's that she's too good to people. They would take advantage of her in prison. Inmates would go to her and ask for anything. It might be her last but she would give it away. We called her "Mother" or "Auntie" because she was just like a house mother.

She'd let inmates sit in her cubicle on her bed for two or three hours and never send them away. I used to say, "Mother, you don't need to mess with her. Why do you let her come up and bother you? Tell her to butt out."

And Mother would say, "Oh, that's all right honey, it's okay."

I used to wonder, "Man, how does she hold up like this?" There are a lot of women in prison doing big time, and they had to get out from under the pressure once in a while. Go off on somebody. Get into an argument. A fight. But Joyce wasn't that way. She carried that pressure inside her and never let it show. It just puzzled me.

Once, though, she lost it.

"Baby," she said, "I'm doing an aggravated life for something I didn't even do. That's twenty years out of my life."

I tried to cheer her up. "Mother, you ain't ever going to do no twenty years. The good Lord knows you're innocent and sooner or later He's going to set you free."

"That's how I make it every day," she said. "People be wondering how I walk around with a smile on my face. I pray every night before I go to bed and every morning when I get up. The Lord is going to let people know I'm innocent."

All of a sudden tears went to rolling down her face, right out of her eyes, and she broke down. We were in the dayroom and no one was in there but me and Mother. And she cried, she cried, she cried. It was one of those hard cries, like she had been holding it in for a long time. She tried to stop herself, but she couldn't. I've seen tears flow out of her eyes on holidays, or special days, but I had never seen her cry that hard. I just wanted to kill the sons-of-bitches that put Mother in there.

–Shirley Nesbitt
Ex-inmate, Mountain View Unit

By the end of 1983, I was happier with myself as a person. There was a certain amount of satisfaction just in knowing that at least the women I lived with had begun to believe that I was innocent of the crime for which I had been convicted. However, that satisfaction could not soften the shock of waking up every morning in a prison cell.

As the year drew to a close, I was given new hope. Lenell Geter became a headline in Texas. Mr. Geter was a black electronics engineer at E-Systems, a defense contractor in Greenville, Texas, located about sixty miles north of Dallas. He had been convicted in 1982 of an armed robbery in the Dallas suburb of Balch Springs. The case against Geter was being established on the strength of a photograph identification by one of the robbery victims and testimony from a Greenville police officer. The defense had countered with testimony from Geter's co-workers that he was at work at the exact time the robbery occurred.

Despite his co-workers' testimony, Geter was convicted. The verdict was based primarily on the photograph identification and on testimony from the Greenville police officer that Geter and several other black engineers who also worked at E-Systems had a reputation of being "bad characters" in Orangeburg, South Carolina, where Geter had attended college. The officer testified that he had talked with a police officer in Orangeburg, but the jury was never told that the Orangeburg officer had denied ever having such a conversation and had even volunteered that Geter was unknown to his department.

Fortunately for Geter, his fellow workers were so outraged at his conviction that they launched a public campaign to win his release. CBS Television's *60 Minutes* became interested in the case and aired a segment that suggested the guilt of another man. They even went so far as to suggest that the Dallas prosecutors *knew* Geter was innocent. A miscarriage of justice was uncovered in less than eighteen months and Geter walked out of prison in January 1984 a free man.

Encouraged by Geter's publicity and release, Kerry filed a writ in my behalf asking the courts to provide me with the same consideration given Mr. Geter. A few days later I was bench warranted from prison back to Dallas where I was to appear before Judge Ron Chapman, who would review my case and determine if I had received a fair trial. My court date was set for January 20.

It all happened so quickly that my spirits went out of sight. I packed my bags and, on the morning I was to leave, I did something I had not done since coming to the Mountain View Unit. I went to breakfast in the dining hall. As I walked through the halls, I was grabbed, hugged, smiled at, wished the best and encouraged by everyone I saw. It was as if the other inmates were as excited about my good fortune as I was. Again, the prison grapevine knew things before the actual parties involved, because many commented on the fact that "both of you will set the record straight."

"Both of you"? Who else could set my record straight? Then at breakfast, I learned that Rene Taylor was also traveling to Dallas—with me! In the months we had spent together at Mountain View, I had never so much as been in the same room with her. Now we'd be riding together for three hours. I didn't particularly look forward to the experience, but her presence made me feel even more confident. It must mean she was ready to tell the truth and the truth would set me free. You can imagine how excited I was.

Leaving prison is just as bad as arriving. I was shackled with leg irons and handcuffs. Instead of being loaded onto that foul-smelling white bus, however, Rene and I were placed in the back seat of a car.

We had very little to say to each other. One, I had no desire to make small talk with the woman who had caused me four years of grief. Two, I couldn't take my eyes off the road.

Something as simple as riding in a car had become terrifying. It had been three years since I had ridden in an automobile, and I was convinced the woman driving the car would get us killed before we could get to in Dallas. I was fidgeting and shifting around so much that Rene finally looked over at me and said, "You're going to make her have a wreck. You're being a back-seat driver. Be cool."

A thought ran across my mind. "If wasn't for you, I wouldn't be in this damned car in the first place." But knowing she wasn't totally responsible, I kept my thoughts to myself. Finally I forced my eyes shut and fell asleep. I woke up when we reached the Dallas county jail.

Lew Starret Jail, as the new facility was called, had been built while I was at Mountain View. From the outside, it looked like a pretty building, but once inside, I quickly discovered that it was still a jail.

Let me pause a moment to explain this procedure. A "bench warrant" is an order from a judge ordering the sheriff to pick up a prisoner at one of the Texas state prisons. When that individual is picked up and returned to Dallas, he or she is processed through the county jail and then, since the inmate is already serving a sentence, transferred to another jail, the Government Center, and is housed there until the appearance before the judge. I knew, from having talked to other inmates who had been on bench warrants, that it would take anywhere from nineteen to twenty-four hours to be processed through the facility before being sent to the Government Center. We were rushed through in less than five.

Rene and I were immediately placed in separate holding tanks. Even though the facility was new, the same old filth, odor, and oppressive atmosphere had already set in. But I barely had time to feel sorry for myself before I was removed and escorted through the booking process. By the time I was finally admitted, it was late afternoon and I had missed the evening meal.

In county jail, the last meal is served at five o'clock. Anyone missing that meal must wait until five the next morning before being fed. That didn't bother me. I knew from listening to others as I was booked that the evening meal for that day consisted of one bologna sandwich, a paper cup of watered-down Koolaid, and two cookies. I had missed more appetizing meals at Mountain View, and I was so excited at the prospect of getting out that I probably wouldn't have eaten anyway.

However, one of the other inmates asked me if I was going to call for my food.

"No, I don't think so," I replied. "Why?"

"Well, if you don't want yours, I'd like to get it. I haven't eaten since yesterday and I'm mighty hungry."

I walked over to the intercom speaker connecting the tank to the guard station and said politely, "I'd like to get something to eat." I explained that in being processed, I had missed the evening meal.

I was assured that they would check on it, but an hour passed and no food was delivered. The girl who had asked me the favor in the first place had long since given up on it, but I called the guard station again. I was tired of being lied to. I was in the custody of the state and it was their responsibility to feed me. They were going to do just that. This time I asked to speak to the captain on duty.

Within a few minutes someone was at the cell and after I explained to him what had happened, he promised to check and get back with me. Ten minutes later he did, but only to inform me that the kitchen was closed and there was nothing he could do until it reopened the next morning.

Enough was enough. I got on the phone and called my family. With the three-way line, my sister Mary called the captain while I silently listened in. When he told her that I had been fed, I hit the roof. "He's lying!" I screamed into the phone. "I haven't been fed! And I want something done about it!"

Surprised and embarrassed that I was on the line, the captain finally promised that he would see to it that I was taken care of. And I was. Five minutes later, a full twelve hours early, I was on my way out of the Lew Starret Jail and over to the Government Center.

Was I mad? When I walked into the booking room, I was furious. I immediately asked for a grievance slip. I was tired, and by then truly hungry, and determined that I was not going to take any more crap from the Dallas system.

An officer asked, "Are you Joyce Ann Brown?"

"Yes, I am!" I snapped in my nastiest voice.

"We heard what happened to you," the young officer said. She then handed me two of the most beautiful sandwiches I have ever seen— the kind my grandma used to make, with thick hunks of meat, lots of lettuce, and juicy tomatoes. She also handed me an apple and a carton of milk.

I felt like a fool. Like an idiot. I was embarrassed for the way I had talked to her and I apologized.

As soon as I had eaten, I was told to strip. They issued me a jump suit exactly like the one I had worn on my last visit. They also issued me two gray sheets—at one time they were probably white—and a thin mattress which I rolled up into a bulky mass and carried on my back as the guard escorted me to cell No. N-S-11. How do I remember it so well? It was the same cell I had been placed in following my conviction three years before.

During my stay at the Government Center, I found myself immediately and inexplicably involved in one controversy after another. All I had wanted to do was come to Dallas, make my appearance before the judge, present my case, have someone acknowledge that my conviction had been a mistake, and be released to my family. Instead I became, in the eyes of the officers, a "troublemaker."

Perhaps I was.

I remember my first confrontation with the jail staff. I was awakened one morning by an argument between an inmate and a guard.

"You ain't getting any free sanitary napkins, lady. If you have money on the books, you have to buy your napkins from the commissary."

"But that ain't right," argued the inmate.

"Don't matter if it's right. It's the rule. If you have money on the books, you have to pay for your napkins."

I thought, *What the hell does money on the books have to do with providing inmates with their basic necessities?* Since inmates are the responsibility of the system, the system is responsibile for taking care of their basic necessities. And in my opinion, sanitary protection definitely qualifies. So, even though I didn't need any, I asked for them to make sure I had heard right. Sure enough. I was informed that since I had money on the books, I had to purchase the item.

Not me. I asked to speak to an officer.

When the lieutenant came to the tank, I asked him, "What's going on? Why are we being denied our supplies?"

He tried to give me some lame excuse that the inmates were "misusing" the sanitary napkins.

"Listen," I told him. "I'm back here on a bench warrant and I have money on the books, but I expect to receive whatever I need and I *don't* expect to pay for it."

The lieutenant conferred with his superiors, the policy was immediately reversed, and all the inmates began to receive their necessities again—free.

Next I got myself tangled up in a jail-wide food controversy. At first, I really didn't pay much attention to the food served in jail. I had never eaten the food served in prison, preferring to buy what I needed from the commissary. County jail was no exception, especially since county jail food is even less appetizing than prison food. For one thing, meals in the county jail are not served in a dining hall. The meals are brought up to each jail floor in trays on a cart. The trays of food are then passed through a small opening into each tank. Theoretically, these carts keep the food warm but more often than not, the warmers units don't work. Sometimes the food is so cold that by the time a tray is passed into the tank, grease has congealed on top of the food. But since I had my own food from the commissary, I didn't pay much attention.

However, one day an inmate walked up to me after she received her tray and asked, "Joyce, what can we do about this?"

I looked at her plate and nearly gagged. Cooked right into the food was a cockroach. I just got furious. Everywhere I turned, I or another inmate was being treated like an animal. The tray she held out to me looked like someone had ground up some horse meat, thrown some tomato sauce over it, added a cockroach or two, and said, "Feed it to the dogs."

I was tired of being one of the dogs.

I looked at the inmate and said, "I'll tell you what we can do about it. We won't accept it. We'll let them know that we want something else and we want it hot."

We quickly spread the word and no lady would accept another tray. The officer tried to bluff everyone with a few threats, trying to get at least one inmate to accept a tray. By getting just one person to accept a tray, he would have technically fulfilled his obligation to feed the tank.

Soon a lieutenant came down and began to question all the inmates, hoping to find that someone had been coerced or forced into not accepting the food. Again, all the women stood their ground. The lieutenant stood there for a moment and then yelled out, "This is your last chance, ladies! Eat now or don't eat at all!"

It got so eerily quiet that, as one inmate later put it, "You could hear a rat piss on cotton." Finally, the officer left. The women looked at me and asked, "What do we do now, Joyce?"

First, I had one group of ladies get on the pay phones to their families and ask them to light up the jail switchboard with complaints, letting the jail officials know that the public was being informed. We had to get those calls out fast because once the jail found out the inmates were raising hell, they would cut off the phones. Then it was time to use the underground telephone system. Remember the toilet pipes? The women flushed the water out and got a message to the men about what was going on.

So far, so good.

Then we began yelling, "Feed us!"

"We want decent food!"

"We want hot food!"

"We want food without roaches!"

Below us, we could hear the men joining our fight. "Feed the women! Feed the women! Feed the women!"

And we were fed.

They brought in what looked like fifty pounds of thickly sliced lunch meat, loaves of bread, cookies and punch. The officers called me to the window and said, "Miss Brown, see that everyone is fed."

The next day, a black chaplain came to see me. My pastor, Reverend Travis Lee, had asked him to check on me. After introducing himself he said, "Joyce, they have labeled you a leader and they don't like leaders. They would have put you into lock-up but they're scared to."

The reason they didn't put me in "lock-up" (an isolation cell) was because I was being interviewed daily by members of the media. Local newspaper, television, and radio reporters were covering my presence in town for the hearing, and the jail officials were afraid I would tell what was going on inside the county jail. They should not have been worried. All I wanted to do was go to court.

A few days later, at 6 a.m. on January 20, 1985, my name was called. "Joyce Ann Brown. Down and out."

It was time to leave the tank and be escorted to the courthouse. I said a prayer, took a deep breath, and headed for the tank exit. I was nervous, but I also had this confident feeling that soon my nightmare would be over. Maybe as soon as tomorrow I would be back home with my family. It wasn't that I had new faith in the system; it was simply inconceivable to me how anyone could fail to recognize the fact that I was innocent.

I was held in a courthouse holding tank for what seemed an eternity. This time the filth didn't phase me because I kept telling myself that this was it. Never again would I be shackled and locked in and forced to breath this sickening air. Hang in there, Joyce. Just a little while longer.

Finally, Kerry showed up.

In the three years since I last saw him, I had always been comforted by Kerry's soft voice on the phone, and by the memory of his shy smile. I was shocked to see him now. His hair had turned from a beautiful dark brown to almost a solid gray. He saw me staring and smiled that shy smile. "For every three gray ones, Joyce, two of them belong to you."

We laughed and talked for a few minutes. Then he left to check on the proceedings. I gathered my things and got myself ready to go. A few minutes later he returned. "We've had to postpone the hearing."

My heart stopped. I stopped breathing. For just a second, I was a dead woman.

"It's all for the good of the case, Joyce," he said quickly.

How could any postponement be for the good of my case? Good would be getting out of this cell and going home. I could feel the resentment and helplessness welling up inside of me, but I was determined to take it like a woman. I just stared at Kerry, dry-eyed, and tried to listen to his explanation. To this date, for the life of me,

I have no idea why we had to postpone that hearing. I don't remember a word of what he said.

Back in the Government Center, the ladies on my floor were waiting to see what had happened. So before I walked with the officer back to 10-S-11, I squared my shoulders and put a smile on my face as if I didn't have a care in the world.

As I expected, everyone was waiting on my return. When the guard opened the door for me, I was surrounded by the women in the tank, each wanting to know what had happened to "Mother." Some were absolutely sincere and caring in their curiosity; others really didn't give a damn but pretended to be interested in order to stay in my good graces. I explained as best I could and then, totally exhausted, climbed into my bunk to think and sleep—but mostly to think. I shut out all the screaming and yelling and hollering and bickering. I turned it off, closed my eyes, and tried to understand why God was putting me through this ordeal.

That postponement was to last six months. Six months of waking up in the county jail every morning, wondering if today was the day. I slept those months away. I slept and slept, and when I could not sleep another wink, I got up and cleaned. County jail cells and tanks are notoriously filthy, but during my stay in the Government Center, MaDear's influence took over. And when I started cleaning, the other inmates, one by one, began to help. Within a short time our quarters became more bearable.

The only other positive note during those six months was being able to use the telephone and have visitors every day. Without those regular conversations and visits with my family, I could not have endured my stay. Yet they only compounded my feelings of self-pity.

At long last, my court date arrived.

That day in court was a study in conflicting emotions. I was seated at a table, facing the judge, and by turning my head slightly, I could see my daughter, mother, sisters, and friends. I had known in advance that Lee Jr. could not make the trip into town that day, but everyone in town had taken time off from work or school to be there. To be so close to them yet so far away was excruciating. My emotions were identical to what I had experienced during the trial. Just as I had then, I longed to reach out and reassure my daughter, hold my mama, thank my brothers and sisters for seeing me through all of this. But our justice system speaks out loud and clear, "Joyce, you're not human. You're a convict, so you can't hug and kiss your family like other humans."

Still, sitting quietly at that table, I believed that the system would admit it had made a mistake and set me free. I really believed it. And as I listened to Kerry present our arguments, that belief and confidence grew.

Once again, people took the stand to testify on my behalf. Mr. Wayne Baker, who had conducted a polygraph test on me shortly before the hearing, testified that based on the results of that test I was innocent. From other inmates I had heard of his excellent reputation and when Mr. Baker said he was convinced of my innocence, I wanted to jump up and scream for joy.

But the most encouraging testimony came from Rene Taylor.

She was called to the stand and, under oath, stated that she had never met me before the crime, did not know me at the time of the crime, and had never met me or heard of me until she had been arrested, months after I had already been convicted. More importantly, Rene testified clearly that I was not the black woman who was her accomplice. When asked to reveal who her accomplice was, she would only admit that it was a woman she knew as "Delores."

Prior to my hearing, Rene had consented to take a polygraph test, and the gentleman conducting the test now stated under oath that the results supported her testimony. According to his findings, she had not known me prior to the crime and I had not been her accomplice.

I knew I was home free.

Finally, after Kerry had presented his argument, the judge sat there for a moment, thinking. My heart started racing. What was he waiting for? What did he have to think about?

Then, he spoke: "I'll go over all the evidence and give my decision at a later date."

What do they think I am? What do they think I'm made of? Iron? My hopes had been built up and then smashed. I kept thinking, *I'm human! Why can't they treat me like a human being?*

I forced the tears back. If they wanted to see me break, they had another think coming. I would not let them know I was breaking apart inside. As I was escorted from the courtroom, I turned around, looked back at my family and gave them the "I'm O.K." smile.

On my way back to that filthy holding tank, I prayed. *Lord, you said that I'm your child. You said, ask and it shall be given. I'm asking that you give me the strength to face the fact that all my dreams won't come true at this time.*

I didn't have to wait in the holding tank long before Kerry showed up, smiling and trying to look encouraging for my benefit. I knew better. He was there to give me me another shock.

"Joyce, when the judge hands down his decision, even if he rules in your favor and decides that you should be granted a new trial or have the case dismissed, it still has to go to the Court of Criminal Appeals. That means we will still have to wait another two or three months on their decision."

When the system is going after a conviction, the wheels can turn so fast your head swims. But to reverse one, the wheels grind down to an agonizing crawl.

I had a decision to make. I could stay in Dallas county jail and wait for the decision of both the judge and the Appeals Court; I could stay and wait on the judge's decision and then go back to Gatesville to await the Appeals Court's ruling; or I could return immediately to T.D.C. to await both. I elected to return to Mountain View. At least I would be able to breathe and lead a more normal life—as normal as I had come to know it, anyway.

Kerry promised to arrange for my transfer. He gave me one more smile, put his hand on my shoulder, and said, "Keep the faith, kid." Then he walked out and left me alone.

That night, I explained everything to my family and said goodbye. I would miss talking to them every day, but the filth and noise of the county jail was more than I could handle.

Now that my decision had been made, I could only sit and wait to pull chain. Once again, I would have to ride that stinking white bus to prison, wearing my state-issued bracelets and anklets, but at least I would have some semblance of hope to comfort me on the trip. Sooner or later they would have to set me free.

On the afternoon before I left, during visiting hours the window flew open and one of the ladies hollered to me, "Joyce, you have a visitor and it's a nice-looking young man!"

I got up from my bunk and walked over to the visitor's window, expecting to see my brother. But a quiet young voice said, "Hello, Mama."

It was Lee Jr.

And Koquice was him.

Both my children.

I had only talked to Lee Jr. on the telephone while waiting in county jail. While I was in prison, he had moved from his grandmother's to live with his dad, Lee Sr., who at that time was living out of state. My only contact with him since returning to the county jail had been on the telephone. Suddenly, he was there to see me. Thank God for that day of pleasure.

We sat and talked and kidded each other. How I wanted to reach through that small window and hold him, kiss him, feel his young strength and growing body. I laughed with joy as he and Koquice argued with each other, as brother and sister always do, each urging me to give the other a spanking—and laughing because they knew I couldn't and wouldn't ever spank either of them.

All too soon, the visit ended. I fought back tears as I told each of them, "I love you, Lee. I love you, Koquice."

"We love you, Mama," they said in chorus.

I watched them walk slowly away, watched as they turned to give me a goodbye smile and a wave, watched as they disappeared from my view. "Goodbye, my babies!" I cried, though I knew they could no longer hear me.

It was the last time I saw my Lee Jr. alive.

8

Happy Birthday, Joyce

Joyce Ann was something very special, not only to me but to the other inmates and prison officers as well.

I remember once, when I worked in the kitchen, an inmate received a message from Joyce Ann telling her that she needed to report to the E&R building to fill out some forms.

The inmate immediately left her job, reported to Joyce Ann, completed the paperwork, and returned to the kitchen. The officer in the kitchen was dumbfounded that the inmate had left her job without permission and was going to give her a case for being out of place. But the inmate explained, "Joyce Ann told me to report to her office."

The officer just shook her head and said, "Oh, that's different." And she didn't write the inmate up.

That's the way Joyce was. She commanded so much respect in prison, even the officers sometimes forgot that she also was an inmate.

–Shirley Young
Former Inmate, Mountain View Unit

A few days later, I stepped off that filthy white bus to see the front gates and barbed wire fences of Mountain View before me. Three years earlier I had arrived here for the first time, full of hatred and bitterness. Some of that bitterness still remained, but mostly I felt only helplessness, despair, and gloom. I looked around and thought, *God, am I ever going to get rid of this place?*

I knew I had friends at Mountain View, but until the day I came back I never realized how many. From the moment I walked through the gates, I could sense genuine love in the greetings I received from prisoners, officers, and guards alike. The sincerity of their feelings helped ease the disappointment I felt at having to return. As I walked to the count office, people came out of their offices to give me a smile, a welcome, a word of encouragement.

It's the count office that gives an inmate her official "Move Ticket," which tells her her dorm and job assignments. When I got mine, I let out a big sigh of relief. I was headed back to the same asignments I had before my bench warrant. At least I would be returning to my close friends and to a job I enjoyed.

"May I go by the office and see my supervisors?" I asked the guard.

"Certainly," she said, smiling.

When I entered the education building, I was greeted with so much kindness that even though I hated the thought of being back, I felt that these people really cared about me. Especially Mr. S. and Madame Butterfly. They were waiting for me with great big smiles of welcome.

Mr. S. gave me one of those big grins of his and shook my hand. Madame Butterfly put her arms around me and said softly, "Joyce, I'm sorry things didn't work out for you, but don't give up hope."

I had cried on their shoulders so much in the past, but this time I kept my composure. I didn't want anyone to think I was a wimp. It seemed like if I broke down, with everyone watching to see how I handled this latest setback, my life would be over. I was already close to becoming a candidate for the Mountain View Psychiatric Center. So I was determined not to give anyone reason to pity me. I wanted help, not pity, and the help I needed couldn't come from these two friends who worked for T.D.C.

It was a day I was glad to see end. By that night, my forced smile was wearing out. So many officers and inmates came by to say hello and to ask how I was doing, that I reached a point where I could not smile and say "I'm doing fine" one more time. Finally it was ten-thirty and the dorm officer yelled, "Lights out, ladies!" That's when the tears started flowing. My entire body was covered with sweat from crying so hard.

As I cried, I heard a whisper from the cubicle next door. "Joyce, are you all right? Do you need to talk?"

"No," I whispered back. "I don't need to talk."

But I did need to talk. I needed to talk to God, and I did.

Nothing at Mountain View had changed. Inmates were still loving inmates; there were more stories of how officers, male and female, were still making it with inmates; and the fighting and bickering resulting from these love affairs still prevailed throughout the entire prison. I could not believe all that was going on, nor could I believe how many officers were hiding their heads in the sand, ignoring what was taking place.

The Mountain View Unit, as is true of most prison units in their locales, is a major industry in the small town of Gatesville. It's the town's largest employer, and the monthly payroll plays an important part in the town's economic well-being. It is not at all unusual for family members or neighbors to work together at a unit—often on the same shift and, in some cases, even in the same department. The prison is their major source of livelihood. They won't do anything to jeopardize a family member's or a neighbor's job.

Consequently, things go on inside our prison that the front office, the high-ranking officers, and the general public never hear about. On rare occasions when atrocities do come to light, punishment from the authorities takes the form of dismissal, a reprimand, or simply a transfer to another unit. I'll leave it to you to guess which "punishment" is usually handed out.

In any environment, there are good people and bad people. So it is within the prison staff. By good, I do not mean guards who let you get away with things; to me, a good guard is one who comes to work, does her or his job in a professional manner, and treats inmates with a certain amount of respect. Some of the very toughest officers in the prison are the most respected, at least by me, because although they are strict, they are fair.

For the most part, I tried to avoid those for whom I had no respect. When I couldn't avoid them, I was polite; but I refused to be intimidated by them. There were only a few that I simply couldn't stand. They were not just bad guards, but despicable human beings, as well.

Ms. Lowlife was one. She may have been the pettiest officer who ever worked at the Mountain View Unit, and her greatest joy seemed to be writing up inmates for the most minor infractions. For example, inmates are allowed to buy hairpins at the commissary, but they can only be used in one's hair. The rule dictates that hairpins cannot be bent or stretched out of shape because that constitutes destruction of state property. But they make great paper clips. Bend one into an L-shape, stick it in the wall, and you have a picture hanger. In prison, where every item is utilized to its fullest, hairpins are often used for these and other purposes. Until she finally left, Ms. Lowlife would hand out cases right and left for the misuse of hairpins, calling it "Possession of contraband."

Once I was helping an inmate with her homework. She was working on math problems dealing with percentages, and in the process of showing her how to do a particular problem, my hand brushed against hers.

Immediately Ms. Lowlife announced, "Ladies, if I see your hands touch again, that's a sex case for both of you."

At first I couldn't believe what she said, and then I just came unglued. I made her call the shift sergeant and when she arrived, I asked her, "If I touch this lady's hand while trying to help her with math, is that a sex case?"

The sergeant looked at me like I was crazy. "Of course not, Joyce. You know better than that."

"Well, I know better, but your guard doesn't know the difference between a hand touch and a homosexual act."

The sergeant talked to Ms. Lowlife and I didn't get a case, but from then on I had to tread very lightly when she was around.

Officers hated to work with Ms. Lowlife and hated it even more when they had to relieve her. She was such a nitpicker and needler. She would send a dorm into constant turmoil, raising tempers to the boiling point. By the time she got off shift, the guard relieving her was faced with the task of neutralizing a powder keg.

Then we discovered Ms. Lowlife's problem. Word began to be spread around the prison that she was a doper. We heard that she would bring her drugs to work and shoot up while on duty. One day she took too much dope and passed out—right in the dorm. Shortly after that, we heard that she had been fired—not for using dope, but for lying to get a night off work. Ms. Lowlife claimed she had to go out of town to look after her son who had been in an automobile accident. But what she really did was go out on a date to a nightclub. Other officers saw her there, and she was dismissed. Moral: If you're a guard, you can do almost anything, but never, *never* inconvenience the prison officers by disrupting the work schedule.

Remember Peggy Sue? The inmate who was involved with Love Child? Peggy Sue got herself involved with yet another guard who, it was rumored, not only used drugs but smuggled them in for inmates as well. They had some kind of a lover's quarrel, so Peggy Sue proceeded to get even. She snitched on this guard to a lieutenant, telling him about an upcoming drug drop.

The story goes that at the designated time, the guard walked past the chapel, paused at the butt can near the door, and concealed a small package in the sand. Nearby, the lieutenant was watching and taking pictures. Confronted with the evidence, the guard had no choice but to admit her guilt. Remember that many of the people in prison are there on drug charges. But rather than being arrested, charged, and convicted, this dope-smuggling guard was asked to resign. To me the moral was: If a guard breaks the law, the prison will take care of it so the free world won't know what's going on.

If there was one guard I absolutely could not stomach, it was Hamburger. As you know, inmates are subject, at any time, any place, to a search by any guard. Each time an inmate leaves a dorm and returns, the search is automatic. Some guards dislike this practice as much as the inmates, but it's their job and they do it in a professional manner. Usually the search consists of a simple "pat search" which involves the guard patting the inmate in places an item will most likely be concealed. However, if the guard has reason to suspect that an inmate is carrying contraband, a more thorough search—even a strip search—can be conducted. There are some who take great pleasure in conducting these searches. Such a woman was Hamburger.

A day never went by that Hamburger didn't find some excuse to conduct a *thorough* search of a prisoner. Inmates were helpless victims of her lustful hands. Any complaints were defended by Hamburger claiming she suspected the inmate of concealing contraand. There may have been a few who enjoyed Hamburger's little sex game, but most of us hated it.

Hamburger would start with your shoulders, bring her hands over your breasts, cupping each one, then down around your ribs. She'd feel her way down over each leg, finally bringing her hands up between your legs. If you were wearing a skirt, she would casually fondle your private area, again using the old concealed contraband bit to justify her actions.

Once, on visitor's day, I bounced down to the visiting room, looking forward to seeing my mama and daughter. Inmates live for visits and mail. Seeing someone you love or receiving a letter is as wonderful and memorable as being wined and dined by a handsome, charming man.

Prison rules dictate that an inmate must be searched before entering and after leaving the visiting room. We are usually given a quick pat search before, and a complete strip search afterward. But that day, as I walked into the clearing room with another inmate, my spirits sank. Hamburger was on duty.

Hamburger started with the other inmate, giving her a simple pat search. When it was my turn, she gave me a nasty grin and proceeded to violate all the good feelings I had been enjoying as I looked forward to my visit. She started with my shoulders, cupped my breasts, and then came down the front of my skirt, pausing at my private area. At that, I did something an inmate is never, never supposed to do: I slapped her hand away.

She was so shocked, she just stood there staring at me. I stared right back. Finally she kind of grinned and said, "Well, I guess you're not hiding anything. You ladies may go on and see your visitors."

Throughout my visit with Mama and Koquice, I kept my smile on, refusing to let them know what had happened, and trying not to think about what was in store following the visit. The time passed all too quickly and finally we had to say goodbye. They left and I returned to the clearing room where Hamburger was waiting. Following the rules, she made me strip my clothes, grinning her nasty little grin as she explored by rectum for contraband. Standing there naked in front of that bitch was almost more than I could handle but, as always, I bit my tongue, smiled sweetly, and went on my way.

Hamburger had another infuriating habit. In the dorm, she would station herself near the showers, so she could stand and stare at the naked ladies showering or using the toilet. You could take a shower, step out of the stall, and there would be Hamburger, her eyes burning a hole in your body. You couldn't help but feel dirty again.

Then one day I learned through the grapevine that she was being considered for promotion to the Education & Recreation building as a security officer.

Over my dead body.

I went to Mr. S. and explained the problem I had been having with Hamburger. He listened sympathetically and promised to look into the matter.

But I wasn't about to take any chances. I dug out the qualifications for the job, trying to discover some technicality that would keep the unit's most aggressive lesbian guard out of my department. As I read the job specifications, I suddenly remembered something. She could not *swim*! I had her. During the summer, when the swimming pool is open, the security officer serves as a life guard. If Hamburger couldn't swim, how could she fill the position? But to insure the situation, a more acceptable guard would have to apply for the position.

With two other inmates, Peaches and Janice, I began to search for a guard who would be less disgusting than Hamburger. One day I looked out the door of the E&R building and there she was. Country. So named because she lived on a small farm near Gatesville where she raised cows, goats, chickens, and kids.

I ran outside. "Can you swim?"

She looked at me like I was crazy. "Yes, why?" I explained the problem. I didn't have to say any more about Hamburger than that she was applying for the position. "Joyce," said Country, "I would love to have the job, but I think it's too late."

"No, it's not," I assured her, knowing my supervisor would be more than willing to accept anyone over Hamburger. Country eventually got the job.

After moving into my department, Country was later to nickname me "Mouse." This came after weeks of her checking the candy stash in her desk and observing, "Well, we must have a mouse in the house. There's another piece of candy gone."

I would smile and say, "One of these days we're going to have to catch that mouse."

Hamburger's eventual downfall and surprising dismissal from the unit came as a result of her behavior as the director of a self-help inmate organization. The group was made up of inmates who were dedicated to helping other indigent inmates. We would sell items throughout the prison to raise money, which was used to buy items for them from the commissary. We also used the proceeds to buy such

things as popcorn, punch, sodas, candy, and apples which we dis-
tributed on holidays.

Somehow, Hamburger maneuvered herself into the directorship of
the group. Her aim was obvious to the inmates but apparently not to
the officials. Supervision of the Help Club provides the director with
an opportunity to be alone with inmates for hours on end, no questions
asked. Hamburger took full advantage of those opportunities to
further her homosexual interests.

Finally her interests resulted in more complaints than the warden
could afford to ignore. We heard that when an investigation found
incriminating photographs of Hamburger and an inmate named Too
Tall in Hamburger's B.O.Q. (Bachelor Officer's Quarters), she was
history. No one, officers or inmates, felt any sympathy for her, and
even referred to her "bust" as poetic justice for all the sex cases she
wrote up. One would think that she, as a homosexual, might be
inclined to overlook lesbian relationships. Not Hamburger. Ironically
she ended up a victim of her own lifestyle.

Then there was Big Daddy. He wore his pants like a second skin
and stood in such a way as to leave us no doubt why he was called
"Big Daddy." Needless to say, jokes about him ran through the prison.
Although he was an obnoxious, even obscene eyesore, he was the
source of a lot of hilarious x-rated material.

No one knew he was fooling around with an inmate. We often saw
him kidding around with Willie Mae, a very pretty black girl with a
mouth full of gold teeth, but the idea of them being involved never
crossed our minds. She was one of the "warden's girls" whose many
special privileges included a furlough every six months. She was
allowed to leave the prison and visit the outside for a weekend. After
one furlough, she returned to prison sporting a brand new watch and
ring. And that's how we found out about Big Daddy and Willie Mae.

Women are jealous creatures. What's the old saying? Never tell a
woman a secret? Especially not in prison. Willie Mae confided to one
of her buddies that Big Daddy had given her the watch and ring. As
a warden's girl, she also enjoyed the privilege of wearing the items
back in the prison even though she had not left with them. Her buddy
snitched. In just a few days an investigation was begun.

You would have thought they were after Public Enemy Number
One. We heard that an investigation had discovered that Big Daddy
and Willie Mae had spent several nights in a motel, then gone to
Dallas to visit her family. When the two pieces of jewelry were

officially discovered in Willie Mae's cubicle, the secret was out. She was transferred to another prison unit, and the word was that Big Daddy was allowed the choice of resigning or being fired. I don't know which option he selected, but I do know he is no longer employed by T.D.C.

Although they have the whole free world to choose from, some guards will even get so involved with inmates that they will fight over them. Two officers, a white and a Hispanic, once got into a fight over Evelyn, an inmate. I guess the Mexican officer won the fight because that's who Evelyn ended up with, even after she was paroled.

There are a lot of bad officers in prison—uncaring, selfish, even immoral people who treat inmates worse than they treat their own dogs. But there are also some fine officers, and two of them in particular helped get me through a very difficult time in my life. During the latter months of 1984 and the first few months of 1985, a series of events threatened to destroy my will to live.

In September, 1984, I received a copy of an article from *The Dallas Morning News* which I could hardly wait to read. It was about Judge Ron Chapman's decision regarding my request for an appeal. He had asked the Texas Criminal Court of Appeals to review my case! But as I read on, my excitement quickly turned to disappointment. Judge Chapman had forwarded my writ to the Appeals court without making any recommendation or comment. In other words, he wasn't really sure I deserved a new trial. He was not convinced I was innocent.

Couldn't he see I was not guilty? Didn't he hear Rene Taylor in that courtroom? What about the polygraph expert?

I threw the article down. Okay, so the writ had been forwarded without the judge's recommendation. Surely the higher court would see the injustice of my case and straighten everything out.

A few months later, I was at work when the mail room called to inform me that I had legal mail to pick up. Even though the mail room is only about a hundred yards from the E&R building, that day it seemed like a mile. I was praying all the way. When I arrived, they handed me a big brown envelope from Kerry's office. I opened it, read the letter inside, folded it back together, put it in the envelope, and went back to the E&R building.

I returned to my desk and Madame Butterfly asked if my mail had been important. "No," I muttered, "it was just a letter."

I tried to work, but I couldn't even see. My eyes kept filling with tears and there didn't seem to be enough work to keep me busy. And I felt rotten for lying to Madame Butterfly, something I had never done.

But she knew me so well, she just gave me my space and let me sit there with my thoughts for awhile, getting myself back together. Then I stood up, walked to her desk, handed her the letter, and went into an empty office. When Madame Butterfly walked into the office, tears in her eyes, she found me squatting beside the file cabinet, sobbing.

I don't know how long I knelt there with her arms around me, but finally I realized that Joyce Ann Brown had to get back in control. I stood up, went to the restroom, washed my face, straightened by hair, and returned to my desk.

Madame Butterfly tried to get me to leave work and return to the dorm and rest, but the best thing for me at that moment was work. I tried to work. But I couldn't keep my mind on anything except the letter.

In it, Kerry explained that the Court had ruled unfavorably on my case. I would not be granted a new trial. Kerry was now filing a writ for a Discretionary Review, but I knew that move didn't offer much hope. The hardest part to accept about it all was that Judge Chapman had refused to comment on my innocence or guilt. The court had merely ruled that I did not deserve a new trial, because even though the question of innocence had been raised, the evidence presented in the Evidentiary Hearing could not be used in my defense. It did not matter if I was innocent. Innocence had nothing to do with it.

Let me explain. And I can, because over the last few years, I've become an expert in criminal law. It is important to understand the way our judicial system works, because what happened to me can—and does, more often than you would ever imagine—happen to anyone.

Clarence Darrow, the great trial lawyer, said it best: "A courtroom is not a place where truth and innocence inevitably triumph; it is only an arena where contending lawyers fight not for justice, but to win." As has been documented more and more of late, when this arena is dominated by an overly aggressive or even unscrupulous prosecutor, the result is a judicial victim—like me. Once you've been convicted and sentenced to prison, your chances of being exonerated are very slim.

I had thought that Rene's testimony and polygraph test would make it obvious that I was innocent, but because she wouldn't provide more information about her true accomplice, it didn't qualify as new evidence. I didn't realize that when seeking redress in the appellate courts, innocence or guilt is totally irrelevant. Appeals courts have only one function—to correct legal mistakes made by a judge in a lower court. If you are innocent, yet your attorney is unable to persuade the Appeals court that any errors were committed at your trial, there is no recourse. Nothing, absolutely nothing, can be done to free you unless new evidence indicating your innocence is discovered. No new evidence, no new trial.

Two months went by without word from the Court of Appeals. My birthday was spent waiting for the mail and then waiting for the day to pass so I could wait for the next day's mail.

Ten days later, on February 22, the letter came. The Texas Court of Criminal Appeals denied my Discretionary Review. Happy Birthday, Joyce.

Twenty days later, on March 14, I received another letter. Marqueta, Lee Jr.'s aunt, had written, "Your son Lee shot himself in the head on March 12th, but he's still alive. They took him to surgery and we are now waiting for the outcome. I'm sorry to have to be the bearer of bad news. Please call as soon as you can."

I must have screamed out because suddenly there was a crowd in my cubicle. My friend Joyce K. ran to my side. "Joyce, what's wrong? What's happened?"

She took the letter from my hands, read it, and then asked if I wanted to go make the telephone call.

I guess I was in a state of shock because I didn't know what she was talking about. "What call? What are you talking about?"

"To call about your son."

By then I was crying but I remember saying, "That's not my baby. Lee Jr. wouldn't do that."

Joyce K. took control. She called down to the infirmary for something to calm me down, but they told her there was nothing they could do. Next she called the count office and explained what had happened. The officer told her to bring me to his office.

We walked down there, but as we arrived the officer Joyce K. had talked to was just leaving for the day. I tried to explain to him that I needed to make a telephone call, but I was crying so hard the words couldn't come out. Joyce showed him the letter and he read it. Shaking his head, he said, "She'll have to wait for the chaplain. I can't approve a call."

He began walking out of the building but not before telling us that the chaplain would not be back for two days. I watched that uncaring son-of-a-bitch walk out the door.

Two days. I couldn't wait two days. I needed to find out if my son was still alive. I could hear this pounding noise and I realized that Joyce K. was beating on the captain's door, demanding that someone talk to us.

After several minutes of pounding, a female officer came out, read the letter, and said, "I'll get the captain to take care of everything, Joyce. I'm a mother and I know what you must be going through. Men can be very cold and unsympathetic in these types of situations."

She was true to her word. I was allowed to use the phone, but I couldn't reach anyone. Everybody I called was at the hospital and I couldn't get through there because the nurse answering the phone would not accept a collect call—the only kind of call inmates are allowed to make.

For weeks I was a zombie, going through the motions of working and living, awaiting word on Lee. Every night I would call Marqueta, Lee's aunt. Every night I was informed, "no change." He was still unconscious.

It was then I began to really understand the decency of the people with whom I lived and worked. Most of the officers were caring and helpful. My fellow inmates took care of me as they would a small child. The shift lieutenants made life more bearable by allowing me to use the phone. The chaplain offered his support. Even the people in the infirmary tried to help, but I didn't want their drugs.

Finally, on the night of April 2, Marqueta told me he had passed the crisis and it appeared he would be all right. I was so happy. I thanked God for his blessings. I could feel the joy in my entire being. I could even smile again.

But a few days later a letter came from Marqueta. Swelling in Lee's brain had developed. I called immediately and was told, "The swelling is under control. They are watching him closely. Everything is fine."

The next morning, April 5, I was awakened around mid-morning. I assumed I had a visitor, but when I walked up to the officer in the pipe chase, she said, "Joyce, you need to report to the chaplain's office immediately."

I couldn't move. Without being told, I knew.

As I left the dorm, I passed Country. She could see the tears in my eyes and she asked, "Joyce, what's wrong?"

"I've got to go to the chaplain's office."

She put her arm around me and guided me through the maze of people who had already learned through the grapevine what had happened and escorted me to the chaplain's office.

When the chaplain looked at me, I knew it was the truth.

Only the fact that Country's arm was around me kept me from falling down. She literally held me up. "I don't believe this is happening."

"Joyce, do you want to be alone? Do you want me to pray with you?"

Sensing my need to be alone, Country guided me out of the chapel and over to the E & R building. There, in one of the offices, I cried on her shoulder as she held me, giving me comfort in the moments when I no longer wanted to live. This was the final blow. There was nothing more that could happen.

Or so I thought.

The prison authorities figured out another way to remind me that I was less than a human being. They refused to grant me permission to attend my son's funeral. I was doing a life sentence and so was ineligible for a furlough—despite the fact that I had spent four years in prison without one rules infraction.

Officers throughout the prison, upon learning my furlough had been denied, volunteered to be my guard and escort me to the funeral at no charge to the state. Not only did they offer to work for free, but to foot all the expenses as well. Denied.

Lee was buried on the afternoon of April 12, 1985.

On that day, shortly after noon, I received a note from the chaplain, asking me to report to the chapel. I expected him to tell me he had learned that it was a nice service and that Lee Jr. had been laid to rest.

I walked into the chapel and he said, "Joyce, God has put you on my mind today. I want you to sit with me."

We spent the next hour reading the Bible and praying together. It was a funeral service for my benefit. During that quiet hour with God and the chaplain, I could not help but recall Lee Jr.'s last words the night he visited me in the Dallas county jail. "Mama, when are they going to let you out? We don't have a family anymore."

Later I learned that the hour we spent together in the prison chapel coincided exactly with the hour of Lee's services which were being conducted hundreds of miles away. I also learned it was the first time the chaplain had ever invited an inmate up for private services for a loved one. My trials and tribulations seemed to have no end—but neither did my blessings.

9

Learning to Let Go

Joyce concealed her feelings from everyone. If we had not been so close, I never would have guessed how rough it was on her after Lee died. There was nothing I could do except just be there. I knew she had to get her mind off what had happened, so I reminded her that it was time to get back to work on obtaining her freedom. And I guess she listened to me because the next thing I knew she was again all wrapped up in the task of finding someone who could help her get out of prison.

–Joyce Logan
Inmate, Mountain View Unit

In the days that followed, Lee's presence was with me through each day. I recalled, in agonizing detail, everything he and I had ever done together. Each night I would fall asleep and each morning wake up overwhelmed by sadness and anger. A young life, just wasted. He would never feel the sun or rain on his face again, never know the thrill of athletics, never experience the joy having his own son.

Let go, I would tell myself. But in thoughts I could stay close to him. I didn't want him out there alone. Oh, how I hurt for my lost son. For more than a month I carried that burden, making myself sick with grief.

Finally, I realized I couldn't continue that way. I couldn't just give up on life so easily. I had a fight with the justice system to finish and I was not ready to give it up. But where could I turn? Who could offer hope of freedom now that the state appeals process had failed me?

Then I remembered Lenell Geter. He was innocent of the crime he had been accused of and had fought the system and won. Surely he would have some advice for me.

I pulled myself together and got busy writing. I sent Geter a letter and included all the newspaper clippings I had concerning my case and conviction. Within a week he wrote back, full of encouragement and ideas. His letter mentioned several organizations working to free innocent people from prison. I wasted no time getting letters off to them.

I sent out eight letters, but received only two responses. One was from an organization called Centurion Ministries and the other was from a group known as People's Court. The letter from Jim Mc-Closkey, director of Centurion Ministries, was straightforward but disappointing. His organization was very small and unable to help me at that time. My case would be retained on file, however, so I might hear from him again. In other words, thanks, but no thanks.

People's Court asked that I forward all information concerning my case. Excited, I promptly sent copies of everything I had. But their response was even less encouraging than Jim McCloskey's. Because of my prior arrest for prostitution, their lawyers had decided it would not be in their best interest to aid me in my struggle for freedom. However, they would welcome support for their organization from my family in the form of a contribution.

I couldn't believe it. In one sentence they told me to get lost and in the next they were asking for money.

I was not about to give up. Next I wrote to *60 Minutes.* Their reply was quick. Although my case seemed to have merit, they would be unable to feature me on the program because of a lack of public interest. I had to agree. Who would be interested in a little Miss Black Nobody screaming "I'm innocent!"?

I couldn't think of where else or who else to write to. Dejected, I sat down and wrote to Kerry. I needed some assurance that all hope was not lost.

He wrote back and encouraged me with the news that he was appealing to the Federal Court for a review of my case. I accepted that and tried to relax. What else could I do? I had failed in the avenues suggested by Lenell Geter, and could do nothing to help Kerry with the appeal. Once again, it was pray-and-wait time.

I knew I wasn't the only one waiting. It was especially rough on Koquice—she was sixteen years old, without her mother, and always having to explain where I was and why. I once asked her how she explained my predicament and she said simply, "My friends know the whole story, and I don't talk about it to anyone else."

There wasn't much I could do for her behind bars, but I did make her promise not to feel guilty about missing the regular weekly visit anytime she had a school function or date. I wanted her to have some semblance of a normal, healthy teenager's life, without the burden of a mandatory visit. So when several months went by and she had not come down to Mountain View with other members of the family, I was glad to think she was busy with school activities.

Then my little sister Tangila came to visit. Tangila had gotten married while I was on bench warrant, and often came to see me with her husband, Dennis. During those visits, she had joked about how I had better hurry up and get out in time to take care of her baby. When she came to visit me back at Gatesville, she was very pregnant and still joking about how I had to get out soon to help her. One day while we were joking about this she said, "You sure are going to be a young granny."

I corrected her. "I'm not going to be that baby's granny. I'll be the auntie or the godmother, not the granny."

But she said it again. "Yeah, you're going to be the youngest granny ever."

"What are you talking about, girl?" I asked. "I'm not going to be a granny."

Suddenly, Tangila mumbled something about needing to get a soda. When she returned, we began talking about something else. I didn't push the conversation because, deep down, I didn't want to know what she was trying to tell me.

Then I got a letter from Koquice.

> *Mama, I have something to tell you and I hope you*
> *don't get mad at me. I just found out that I am*
> *pregnant. I know you think I'm too young to have a*
> *baby, but I'm not. I'll be down this weekend to talk to*
> *you about it, but I want you to know that everything*
> *is going to be all right. Also, I know how important it*
> *is to you for me to finish high school, so I promise you*
> *that I will finish with my senior class. I will graduate.*
> *And I will have this baby.*
>
> *I love you so much mama. Don't be too mad at me.*
>
> —Koquice

I took a deep breath. If only I had been home, I never would have allowed this to happen. But happen it did, so I prepared to encourage and help Koquice as best I could with her pregnancy and motherhood.

Finally Koquice came to see me. She walked into the visiting room wearing a sweatshirt that read "BABY IN '86" with a big arrow pointing to her little tummy. I just wanted to grab my baby and hold her. Instead I sat down, looked through the chicken wire, and smiled at her and MaDear.

Today I would give the world for my grandbaby, but at that time, sitting across from Koquice, I could only feel sad and hurt—a feeling that I had let Koquice down. My mind was running wild with with the realization that I wasn't going to be there in the delivery room when the baby was born. I wouldn't be there to share all the things with her I had learned from MaDear about changing diapers, feeding babies, and singing the old gospel hymns to put them to sleep. I knew they wouldn't give me a furlough, so I could only smile and listen to her excited plans.

All too soon, our visiting time was up. Koquice looked at me and said quietly, "Mama, I will graduate from high school with my class."

"I know you will, baby. And I want you to know I love you and I'm proud of you."

Her eyes began to fill with tears and she said, "Mama, my baby is not a mistake. I need something of my own to love, and to love me. I wanted to get pregnant."

I knew what she was telling me. Her mother was in prison, her brother was dead, and she was alone. I interrupted her. "I understand, and this baby is not going to be called a mistake. What is, is and we accept it right here and now and go forward."

Then I looked at MaDear, who had sat listening to us in silence. Before the guard could rush me out I said to her, "You take care of my babies."

On February 6, 1986, the warden sent word that my sister Mary had called to report that I was the grandmother of a beautiful, light-complected, seven-pound girl, Brittany Emia. "Mother and baby are doing fine."

One month later, I got to see my granddaughter for the first time. I'll never forget that day. I was a nervous wreck.

I paced the floor of the dayroom, waiting for my name to be called to report to the visitor's room. I twisted my hands, fiddled with my scarf, adjusted my hair, made sure my face was made up all right, and paced the floor some more. My friend Barbara was waiting for visitors too, and she tried to calm me down, but soon she was called and I was left alone, still walking the floor. Finally, my name was called.

Down in the visiting room, the first person I saw was Barbara, waving her hands and teasing me because she got to see my granddaughter before I did. I didn't care because suddenly I was standing there, looking at my little Brittainy.

Oh God, she was so beautiful! All I wanted to do was reach out and take her from Koquice's arms. But I couldn't. I couldn't lift little Brittainy to rest on my breast. I couldn't put my arms around Koquice. All I could do was stand there, staring through the chickenwire.

The beauty and joy of that moment was scarred by the helpless rage welling up inside me. I might have felt differently if I was standing there guilty of a crime, but I don't know. At that moment, I don't know if it would have made any difference at all.

I didn't cry and I was able to mask the terrible feelings I had inside. For the length of our visit, I forced everything out of my head and heart except the joy of looking at my first grandbaby.

But when I left the visiting room, it all came back. Walking back to my dorm I kept telling myself it was my problem to deal with, no one else's, and I had to maintain. I needed to get back to my room before my temper flew off the handle. It was a very long walk.

People kept stopping me to ask, "How was your visit?"

"Who came to see you?"

"How does it feel to be a granny?"

I could only smile and answer in my most pleasant voice, "It feels great." My only out was my bed.

I lay there for six or seven hours, just thinking. Everybody thought I was asleep which was good because I didn't want to be disturbed. I didn't want to hurt anyone's feelings just because they wanted to help, but by that point, I would have. Finally, I fell asleep.

I woke up sometime during the night feeling like a drunk with a hangover. Although I don't drink, I can imagine how some people try to drink their problems away. I tried to sleep mine away, and the results were the same; when you come to, the problems are still there. Something inside of me had to loosen up so I could come back to my merry self again. That's when I stared at those dull brick walls and prayed for strength.

In moments of despair, I think we put our problems in God's hands and say, "Take care of them for me." But we snatch 'em right back and the burden's on us. And then we pray some more; we tell Him, "I can't take it anymore." So He reaches back down and lifts them, and holds them until we snatch them back again. It's a habit we can't seem to break, snatching our problems back and worrying and worrying about them when there is nothing we can do. It's just human, I guess. I know I couldn't break that habit. I haven't broken it yet.

10

Seasons of Discontent

When you're in prison, keeping some state of high morale is a constant battle. It's a battle an inmate never really wins because, you wake up every morning knowing that today is going to be a repeat of every previous day. The only thing that ever changes are our rules. And those changes are always for some pointless reason.

Such was the case in 1985 when the assistant warden initiated the series of changes which were to bring about a complete disruption of prison routine. Of all the wardens I have seen come through Mountain View, she was by far the most insensitive. Because of her, Mountain View had its first outright rebellion. It was the Riot of '85.

-Ruby Z.
Inmate, Mountain View Unit

So the years passed. The brick walls faded to a duller red, the chain-link fence topped with curlicue barbed wire grew taller, and the routine of "rehabilitation" became even more boringly redundant. It would have been easy to give up, to slip deeper into a pit of self-pity, but I had to keep fighting. There's a little poem in prison,

Two prisoners looked through the bars,
One saw mud, the other saw stars.

I want you to know that sometimes it was very difficult to see the stars.

Rene was still a thorn in my side. My feelings toward her were so mixed. As much as I wanted to hate her, I couldn't. Maybe it was because I knew in my heart that she and her accomplice didn't go out to commit a crime with the intent of framing Joyce Ann Brown. I respected the fact that she had told the truth concerning me. She had consistently maintained that I was not her accomplice. Of course, she could have made my life easier by naming that accomplice.

I couldn't hate her, but I did despise her. I despised her for the cold-blooded crime she had committed. And I despised her for what that crime had done to me. But until I could find another way to prove my innocence, I had no choice but to keep her out of my thoughts. I just put her out of my mind and continued fighting my time in my own quiet way.

Others, however, fought their time in a different manner.

"I'm going to whip me an officer's ass before the day is over."

No one paid any attention to Dorothy, a huge black woman, the morning she made that announcement. It sounded like another typical case of mouth. But that evening, when a young officer entered the dorm to do a head-count, Dorothy grabbed her in a choke hold and began punching her in the face. The guard in the pipe chase could only watch helplessly because, when two officers are on duty, the rules dictate that only one may enter the dorm while the other remains outside with the keys. Even though her fellow officer was being thoroughly beaten up, the pipe chase guard could not leave her post until additional officers arrived. By that time, the one-sided fight was over and the bloody officer was lying on the floor.

She was taken to the unit infirmary and we never saw her again. Dorothy was escorted to segregation where she remained in solitary confinement for more than a year.

Although I and many other inmates didn't respect many of the prison officers, we couldn't help but sympathize with the problems they had to deal with every working day. True, many of their problems are created by their own insensitivity and apathy, but they do have to work in a very tension-filled atmosphere. When trouble erupts, an officer is shockingly vulnerable.

Absolutely nothing in prison creates more problems, more trouble, and more tension than *change*. Remember that when you enter prison your individuality is immediately surrendered. From day one, you cease to be a person. You are a number, another head of cattle. All rights, privileges, and possessions belong to the prison administrators and, by their dictates, are doled out by their officers.

When you have nothing, anything you do manage to obtain becomes ultra valuable. A bottle of perfume is an obscenely treasured prize. A phone call to your family turns into a precious privilege. A small transistor radio becomes an highly valued luxury. These prizes are zealously guarded and any, I mean *any*, infringement or threat to them results in immediate over-reaction.

Once someone slipped into Sally's cubicle and cut the electrical cord on her radio. There is no repair shop in prison. When something is broken or stolen, you simply have to purchase another one. Sally, faced with the prospect of having to purchase another radio that could be destroyed just as easily, requested a transfer to another dorm. Her request was granted and on the day she moved, she quietly snuck into the cubicle of the person she suspected of having ruined her radio. Retaliation time. Sally took a burning cigarette and proceeded to burn holes in as many of the inmate's belongings as she could. "Vengeance is mine," sayeth the inmate.

Equally relevant and just as potentially disruptive is any change in daily routine. Inmates become creatures of habit. Call it institutionalization, boredom, or the desire to have some tiny bit of control over your life. Any change is viewed as an abuse of rights. For example, the lights-out call is scheduled for ten o'clock every night. If for some reason administration should decide to move the lights-out call to nine forty-five, every inmate would immediately become aroused and start yelling for the lieutenant on duty. It becomes hell-raising time.

One day a new order was handed down that I took very personally. Just thinking about it made me seethe. It turned even me into a rebel. What was all the fuss about? Fingernails.

Throughout my entire "visit" in prison, I always exercised special attention to my personal appearance. One of my proudest features was my fingernails. They were long, well-manicured, and always beautifully polished. So when the word came down that inmates could not maintain fingernails longer than one-eighth of an inch, I came unglued. My personal world had been invaded. My personal rights were being violated. My long fingernails were so important to me that I ignored the order and refused to cut them.

After several weeks, the major called me into her office. "Joyce, someone dropped a note to the warden and asked if you were a special inmate because you haven't cut your nails to comply with the new regulation."

I knew immediately who had dropped the note—a white guard we called Albino who had worked a shift in my dorm and was obviously afraid to ask me herself. "Major," I explained, "no one has ever told me I had to cut my nails. I certainly wasn't going to cut them on my own."

The major smiled and said, "Joyce, so we don't have any further problems over this, when you return to your dorm, cut your nails."

I must have had a terrible expression on my face because she added, "Don't run out of here and go cut to them to the quick. Just trim them down a little."

Seemingly insignificant changes like this caused two so-called riots while I was at Mountain View. In 1985, Warden P. retired and her assistant, Warden B., was put in charge. Warden B. initiated a series of changes which ultimately cost her her job. She was a former nun who still believed in the vows of poverty and tried to force her beliefs on the prison population.

First Warden B. rescinded the policy which permitted departing inmates to bequeath their personal possessions to other inmates before leaving. Her new policy stated that all possessions must be mailed home or destroyed. Then she limited the amount of personal belongings each inmate could have and dictated that inmates could retain only two pairs of shoes. Next, she announced plans for decreasing an inmate's bimonthly commissary expenditures from $50 to $10, and for limiting the variety of items the commissary would carry.

It was this last item that finally aroused the inmates' wrath, because one of the commissary items set for elimination was yarn. That's right! Plain old knitting yarn. In its way, yarn is as valuable as money in prison. Inmates, especially poor ones, knit various items of cloth- ing which they sell to other inmates in exchange for commissary items; inmates also use yarn to make gifts for family members in the free world.

The changes provoked anger throughout the prison, particularly in A Dorm. "We just decided we were not going to put up with any more shit," said Ruby Z., an inmate who lived there.

And they didn't.

The inmates tried to contact the warden, but when she refused to discuss the changes, they took matters into their own hands. Late one evening, on third shift, boiling water was thrown on one of the officers. Shrieking, she called her superior. "I've been burned and I'm getting out of here!"

After she left her post to get medical help, all hell broke out in A Dorm. The inmates began yelling, throwing things, and breaking windows. Other officers rushed to the scene and tried to calm the inmates down, but the inmates sprayed them with fire extinguishers and barricaded themselves in the dayroom, shoving furniture in front of the doors.

In retaliation, prison officials locked all doors leading to the dorm and turned off both the water and the electricity. No one could get in, no one could get out. The stalemate went on for a week. The inmates were fed sack lunches through the pipe chase and those requiring medication got it in the same manner. Only one inmate, an elderly woman with a heart condition, was allowed to leave.

On the seventh night, the inmates heard an unnatural silence descend outside the dorm. They felt something was about to happen. Sure enough, just before midnight, a group of guards stormed the dorm, wearing helmets and gas masks, and swinging billy clubs. Their major informed the forty-five inmates that she was going to call out some names and those called were to proceed outside. If they did not comply with the order, further action would be taken.

Six names were announced, and six inmates, still wearing pajamas, reluctantly went outside. They were sent into the cold winter air, loaded into a van, and taken to the other women's unit at Gatesville.

When word spread that six inmates from A Dorm had been taken away, others rebelled. G Dorm barricaded its doors, refusing to allow anyone in or out. Inmates also began demanding to see the T.D.C. director. Surprisingly, he agreed to meet with them and discuss their grievances. He flew in by private helicopter and landed right on the unit grounds.

After conducting a hearing with the inmates of several dorms, he promised to conduct an investigation. True to his word, he checked out the complaints and within a very short time appointed a new warden. For a while, Mountain View got back to normal and the tension eased.

A few years later, there was another major confrontation between inmates and prison officials. It is referred to as the Riot of '89, but it wasn't much of a riot and only involved a small segment of the prison—the inmates in Cell Block.

On June 5, 1989, thirty-seven Cell Block inmates participated in a sit-down and refused to work because they thought the conditions within their living area were intolerable. Their complaints included being the last to go to commissary and not liking the way officers talked to them, among other petty things.

The following day, the rebellion escalated to the point where some of the inmates lit small fires in their cells. Some inmates even began throwing water on the officers—water from the toilets filled with shit and piss.

Late that afternoon, the warden visited Cell Block. "Are any of you ladies ready to end this nonsense and go back to work?"

Although several elected to stop their sit-down, the majority refused.

"I will give you ladies one more chance," the warden announced. "Are any more of you willing to call it quits and cease this disturbance?"

Again, the remaining women refused to give in and elected to remain in their cells. Note that I said "in their cells." Although the women were refusing to fall out for work detail and were guilty of starting small fires or throwing water, they couldn't do much more than that. For the duration of the so-called riot, they were in lockdown—literally locked in their cells.

However, the warden decided not to wait them out. She charged the unit with guards who threw tear gas bombs down the hallway. This effectively ended the rebellion. The so-called rioters were escorted to the gym where they were allowed to shower and wash the gas from their bodies. A few were rushed to the unit infirmary, where they were treated for respiratory or cardiac problems. Some were transferred to the Psychiatric Treatment Center for observation. The entire unit went on lock-down, all privileges were suspended, outgoing mail was slowed down, and inmate phone calls to the free world were suspended. It was several weeks before the prison returned to normal.

Compared to the male units, riots in a women's prison are mild. In general, violence is less intense in the sense that it seldom results in the death of an inmate. But violence does erupt, and often results in serious injuries.

Fights among female inmates can break out for the most trivial of reasons, but most occur as a result of homosexual intrigues or racial slurs. Seldom do fights break out spontaneously. When two inmates become involved in a verbal confrontation or when someone feels she has been insulted, taken advantage of, or wronged, the impulse to lash out immediately is almost always controlled.

Here's what happens when it isn't.

Inmates know that if they fight in the presence of an officer, a case will be issued to each of them no matter who started it. Consequently, most fights are "sneak attacks" that are carried out when an officer is not looking. Retaliation is swift, so even though an inmate may be lying on the floor, knocked out or bleeding, no one gets a case, because the officer did not actually see the fight.

As you might expect, there are officers who despise inmates to such a degree that even though they know something is going down, they will deliberately look the other way so they can later say, "I didn't see a thing."

In other instances, an inmate may pull such a con job on the officer that she indeed never does see it go down. For example, three inmates will conspire to "get" another inmate for some real or imagined offense. Two will go out and get the officer's attention on some pretext. While they distract her with conversation, the third inmate attacks the unwitting victim. By the time the officer realizes something is going on, the fight is over and the attacker is back in her own cubicle, innocently asking, "What's going on?"

I saw this happen a hundred times.

"I'm going to get you, bitch!" one will yell to another.

"You just crank it up anytime, bitch!" the other replies.

More words are exchanged and the officer will finally issue an order to "Hold it down in there, ladies!" The noise ceases but everyone knows it isn't over. Sooner or later, when the officer isn't looking, the fight will erupt, the damage will be done, and *then* things will quiet down for a while.

The most popular time for retaliation is after lights-out. After ten o'clock inmates are supposed to be asleep in their bunks while the officer keeps a vigilant and protective eye over the dorm. Unfortunately, officers like to sleep, too—or read, or work crossword puzzles, or just stare into space. Consequently, a "sleeping" inmate is anything but safe.

A Hispanic woman once felt the need to get even with another inmate for some affront. She waited patiently until the wee hours of the morning. Then while everyone—including the guard on duty—was sleeping, she slipped into the inmate's room. Without warning, she began to beat her with the iron leg of a chair. Before anyone was awakened, she was back in her own bed feigning sleep while her victim lay bleeding and unconscious.

Weapons in prison are easily obtained, easily concealed, and just as easily used. A padlock in a sock serves as a lethal club; a razor blade embedded in a toothbrush makes a slashing shiv; water, heated to a boil on a hot plate, inflicts serious damage when thrown; an iron leg from a chair can kill someone; and a knitting needle is as dangerous as an ice pick.

In all my years behind bars, women were routinely and regularly injured with weapons like these, but unlike the male units we heard about, no woman was ever killed in a fight. In fact, I know of only three women who died during my years in prison. One died of cancer. I would attribute the other two deaths to the apathetic, even negligent attitude of prison officials.

One night, a woman slipped, fell, and hit her head on either the metal bed or locker. As she lay on the floor, not moving, other inmates rushed into her cubicle to see what had happened. They realized that she was seriously hurt and ran to the pipe chase to inform the guard.

When an inmate is hurt or ill, she must obtain a pass to visit the infirmary. This procedure doesn't present any problems during the day when the infirmary staff can handle any patient load. At night or on weekends, however, when the infirmary is manned by a skeletal crew, special permission must be obtained from the pipe chase officer. She must determine if the inmate really needs to go to the infirmary. Keep in mind that guards have no medical training and very little, if any, education beyond high school, and yet they are allowed to determine whether someone needs medical help or not.

"Call the infirmary, we've had an accident!" one of the ladies screamed out.

"Do it quick. It looks serious," another volunteered.

But remember the rule. No officer can enter the dorm unless another one is stationed outside. First, the officer had to call for a "rover," an officer who serves as a back-up guard throughout the prison for those occasions when a pipe chase officer needs to enter a dorm. Getting the rover to our dorm took several minutes, and then more time was wasted while the officer inspected the injured inmate to insure that she was not pulling a con.

Finally she informed the rover. "Better call the infirmary. I think it's serious."

Whenever an inmate leaves a dorm for the infirmary on a pass, she is allowed three minutes to make the journey—three minutes because it has been determined that that is the maximum length of time needed to walk from any dorm to the infirmary. However, from the moment the call was made to the infirmary, the nurse on duty took forty-five minutes to make an appearance. By then it was too late. The inmate was dead by the time they were ready to treat her.

On the second occasion, Mattie, an inmate from E Dorm, reported to the infirmary complaining of a nagging headache. She received the proverbial, "Take two aspirin and call me in the morning."

For several days, Mattie reported to the infirmary each morning with a headache that would not go away. Each morning, she was provided with two more aspirin. One day she even stopped the warden and complained, "Warden, those folks in the infirmary are not doing anything to get rid of these headaches. They're about to kill me and I need some relief." The warden promised to look into the situation.

The following day, Mattie suffered a hemorrhage in her head and had to be rushed to the hospital. You can imagine what the word "rushed" meant in prison. First, standard procedures had to be followed to be sure that she wasn't pulling a con. When it was determined that she truly needed hospital care, a qualified ambulance driver was unavailable. More time was lost trying to locate one. When this proved impossible, the warden decided she would drive the ambulance herself. Before leaving, however, she deemed that it was necessary—with the inmate lying unconscious on a stretcher—to return to the pickett watchtower where officers leave their weapons when entering the prison, find a pistol, and strap it on. Only after that did she return to the infirmary, collect the stricken inmate, and leave.

It was too late. By the next morning, word spread throughout the unit that Mattie was brain dead. She was kept alive on a life-support system for several weeks, but then we received word that the plug had been pulled and she had died.

11

Friends

When I first came to Mountain View, I had what you might call an attitude problem. I didn't like anyone and didn't care if anyone liked me. I was totally negative, and I wasn't too enthused when I was assigned to work in the Count Office, even though I was to be working with the "prison legend," Joyce Brown.

Everyone knew her. She had grandchildren, daughters, and nieces all over the unit and, at first, I couldn't understand why. To me, she was just another inmate claiming to be innocent. Then I got to know her.

She became my mentor, my advisor, my friend; and over the years as I watched her, I think I discovered why Joyce commands so much respect among not only inmates but officers as well.

Joyce is able to do something very few people are capable of doing: she listens to what someone is saying to her. That's right, she knows how to listen, how to hear, how to understand what you are saying to her, and her response is going to be completely honest. It may not be what you want to hear, but it's going to be straight from Joyce's heart.

Joyce is a listener and anyone who really listens is a good friend to have—in prison or out.

–Joni Pearson
Inmate, Mountain View Unit

One of the hardest things about living behind prison walls is seeing your family grow and change without you. The biweekly visits only accentuate your isolation. From behind bars and chicken wire, I watched as Brittainy blossomed into a fiesty little bundle of joy, Koquice matured into a grown woman, and MaDear began to show the inevitable signs of age.

Our family has always been close. Each of us looks to the other for emotional support and everyday companionship. Although they never missed coming to see me, their visits always reminded me of what I was being cheated out of. I couldn't share their experiences on a first-hand basis. I could only listen and comment and watch. That hurt. I could never get over the loneliness of spending year after year without them, but I did find a way to live with it. I eventually developed my own internal family of friends.

The word friendship takes on a different meaning in prison. An inmate has to choose friends wisely and even then, they can abuse you. To begin with, many inmates are not used to real friendship. They come in already accustomed to taking advantage of people, because they're mistrustful and even scared of them. Once inside, they simply continue what they have always done on the outside— getting whatever they can out of their fellow inmates. Friendship becomes a game—a game played by those who don't value a true friend. What many of them never understood was that when you use or abuse a friend, you are really just using or abusing yourself.

Suppose an inmate kisses up to another inmate in order to get that person to spend ten or twenty dollars at the store in her behalf. She might iron that inmate's clothes, clean her cubicle, or do other favors—all in the name of friendship. But it's just really a way of getting something in exchange. Then the inmate will brag about how she got her "friend" to buy her goods from the commissary, making her friend a "trick." I'd try to explain, "No, you're the trick. You performed a service and your friend paid you. So you're the trick, not your friend."

My friends did things for me, but I didn't pay them. Even when they offered to do me favors in exchange for pay, I wouldn't go along. Shawana once came up to me and asked, "Granny, can I iron your clothes and get you to buy some things in the commissary for me?"

I told her no. I said, "Margaret irons my clothes and I don't pay her. If I paid you to iron my clothes, that would make you my maid. Then the first time I couldn't pay you, we'd have a problem. You'd get mad, and I wouldn't get my clothes ironed."

What she couldn't understand was that Margaret ironed my clothes because she was my friend and I did things for her because she was my friend. There were no strings attached. Whatever we did for each other was out of love and concern. I was very fortunate. In addition to the prison-wide network of friends I gained over the years, I also had two true friends, of whom Margaret was the first.

Margaret didn't like me one bit when we met. When she first moved into my dorm she was very shy, just a sweet child (though she's over thirty years old) who would not offend a fly. Because of her gentle nature, inmates walked all over Margaret and took advantage of her. I didn't. But she considered me rude and mean simply because when my opinion is asked, I consider it a disservice to answer with anything other than the truth.

I used to tell Margaret, "If someone has bad breath, their breath stinks and there is no polite way to dress that up. If they have a hygienic problem, they need to correct it. If you don't tell them the truth, you're not helping them." I'd say, "Margaret, if you tell somebody something that's not the truth, it makes you look like a fool." Too many people—especially when they're trying to get something out of you—tend to say what you want to hear. I told it like it was.

I gradually began taking care of Margaret, doing little things for her, and helping her with commissary items. She recognized that I did it for only one reason—because I thought of her as a friend. I didn't have an axe to grind or any ulterior motives. Gradually, by not sugarcoating my comments or advice, I saw her gain more confidence in herself and begin standing on her own two feet.

We never sent our clothes to the laundry because all they did was make our whites dingy. Clothes were not supposed to be washed in the dorm, but we did it anyway. Margaret did all the washing; I did all the cooking and kept the commissary (our food stock) for us.

Margaret's a pretty woman. She has the smoothest skin and the most beautiful eyes you've ever seen. I used to kid her unmercifully about being an alien from outer space because, as I told her, "No woman from this planet could have eyes like that."

And she was a trip. We used to call her Edith Bunker because when she went anywhere—to the sink to wash her hands, for instance—she would run just like Edith did on *All In The Family*, her hands waving in the air. I'd yell out, "Edith Bunker, will you please stop running everywhere you go?"

She'd run to the bathroom, she'd run to the sink, she'd run to her cubicle, and we would just crack up. The only time she didn't run was outside, because it was against the rules. What made it funnier was that Margaret had never even seen *All In The Family*. I don't even know if she knew who the character was, but she was the spitting image of Edith Bunker in every mannerism. We called her "our black Edith Bunker."

As close as I was to Margaret, and I mean we were so close that if she got out of prison today she could move in with my children and me tomorrow, my very dearest and closest friend in prison was Logan.

Joyce Ann Logan is serving a forty-five-year sentence for aggravated robbery. She is several years older than I, and we have known each other since childhood. Before we were teenagers, my sister Mary and I used to visit relatives in a north Dallas project where Logan also lived. We would play softball on the parking lot, and it was there I had my first crush on a boy—one of Logan's six brothers. As we grew older, our paths went in different directions. I didn't see her again until she arrived at the Mountain View Unit in 1983.

At that time, I worked in the writ room. I had volunteered for the job, and it was a good one. Basically, all I had to do was keep the room clean, re-shelve the books used by inmates, and keep the writ files up-to-date and current with the materials T.D.C. forwarded to us. It was boring work, but one day I was sitting there and said to myself, "To hell with this sitting around. Let me find out what's going on." I began reading up on what rights inmates had. I read everything, including all the paperwork from T.D.C., that I had to file. I also began researching cases and found out how to go from one book to another. Every three months the gentleman in charge of all T.D.C. writ rooms would come in to make an inspection and while he was there, he would show me how to use the legal reference books. Before you know it, I got to be known as a "writ lawyer" based on the expertise and skill I had acquired in this area.

It was a good job, though at first there were many days when I didn't show up for work. Until 1986, the writ room was really a love nest for homosexuals. I learned quickly to check the list of those scheduled to visit the room. If the list indicated a couple, I didn't go to work. I just let them alone down there to do their thing. Later on, it became mandatory that an officer be on duty, so that took care of the love nest problem.

And that is where I renewed my friendship with Logan. She started coming in to work on her case, and I would teach her what I had learned about legal research. Within a year, Logan had out-distanced me in her legal knowledge and became what she is today, the unit's "writ writer" or "inmate lawyer."

She also became known as "the nutty professor" because she wears her hair in an afro, has big glasses, and has enjoyed quite a bit of success as a writ writer for other inmates. In fact, the few arguments Logan and I ever had were over the amount of work she did on behalf of everyone else. They would walk in, show Logan what they needed for a writ, then go outside to be "on the rec" (our name for hanging out in the recreation yard) with their people, leaving Logan to pour over dusty legal books.

"Logan, you are crazy to do that."

She'd look up at me with those big brown eyes and say, "But Joyce, they need help."

I'd get so mad. "Yeah, they need help, but they don't want it bad enough to sit in here and help you. You're doing all the work and they're outside socializing."

That didn't bother her. She just continued working on everyone's writs and seldom got around to working on her own.

When I asked her why she didn't work on her writ, she answered, "I get to looking at my case and see how they screwed me and I get so mad I can't work on it."

The first time one of her writs for another inmate received an action she was so happy she couldn't sit still. It was her first success as a writ lawyer and you would have thought it had been in her own behalf. She had many successes, including a civil suit she brought against T.D.C. when she had been wrongly accused of a rules infraction. From then on, everyone turned to Logan for writ assistance in filing grievances against T.D.C.

Even guards and officers came to her, on the qt, to get her help because they knew Logan was good at what she was doing. In the early 1980s, when the federal government challenged the way Texas ran its prison system, the Supreme Court eventually handed down a decision which enabled both inmates and prison employees to file grievances against the administration. Prior to that time, neither inmates nor prison employees had any knowledge of any recourse or procedure in filing complaints against the prison administration. When that avenue opened up, Logan helped the guards file their grievances and complaints against their superiors.

In 1985, Logan was transferred into my dorm. She had a terrible cold and was so dizzy that she could barely carry her things into the dorm. She was a pitiful case, and I set out to take care of her. I made sure she got plenty of hot soup and juices, and sort of mothered her. We were together again and the friendship that had been born as children and renewed in the writ room was re-established—stronger than ever.

> *Joyce Ann Brown is spoiled and she can't deny it. She would cook for me and Margaret and other in-mates, but she rarely made her own bed, never made her own coffee, never did her own hair, never carried her own groceries and commissary items back to the dorm, and actually did very little. Inmates did it for her. She was spoiled. We all spoiled her. I spoiled her because she was my dearest friend. Other inmates spoiled her because she was a one-of-a-kind in prison, a very special woman.*

-Joyce Ann Logan
Inmate, Mountain View Unit

Logan did have one peculiarity that used to drive me nuts. She would get up at 3:00 a.m. every night to go to the bathroom. And every night, at 3:02, her voice would wake me up.

"Joyce? Are you asleep?"

"What do you think I'm doing over here, girl? Of course I'm asleep. What do you want?"

"Joyce, I'm hunggggggggry," she would moan pathetically.

I'd get out of bed, pull out my commissary box, find a snack, throw it to her, and get back in bed.

Finally, I got tired of that. Before I went to sleep at night, I would take out a dozen or so snacks, hang them on the wall, and tell Logan, "Don't you wake me up no more. If you get hungry, you come in here and get what you want—but don't wake me up."

Logan was also responsible for the only time I ever came close to getting into serious trouble in prison. What happened scared me to death.

Logan was once snowed under with a lot of legal typing and no secretary to help her, so I volunteered to give her a hand. The dorm officer gave us permission to continue working in the dayroom after lights out, but the noise of the typewriter disturbed the inmates. We had to move. But where?

We decided to finish our work in the dorm's storage area. The area had a bathroom attached, so we insulated that noisy typewriter even further and set up in there. Logan ran an extension cord from the next room, I put the typewriter on the toilet, and we resumed our work.

Everything was fine until we heard a noise at the front door. That could mean only one thing. The lieutenant was making her rounds. At that time, we had an officer stationed inside the dorm, as well as in the pipe chase. The dorm officer had given us unofficial permission to do our work with the understanding that we not let the pipe chase guard know what was going on. If the pipe chase guard discovered what was happening, all of us would have been in trouble—Logan and I would have received a case (Being out of place) and the dorm officer would have been fired on the spot. Being out of place after lights-out is an automatic case and being out of place in a bathroom with another inmate is the dreaded sex case. If we were caught, there was no acceptable excuse. We were in deep shit.

I turned out the bathroom light and we both pressed up against the wall, in the darkest corner, praying that we wouldn't get caught.

I quickly said a little prayer out loud, "Oh Lord, please don't let us get busted in here and get a sex case."

Logan hadn't even thought about that charge and when she heard me voice my fears, she hit the panic button. She jumped away from me, out of the bathroom, and fell over the bed, making a racket to raise the dead.

"What are you doing, girl?" I whispered.

Logan was so scared, she couldn't even talk. She just stared at me across the room, the whites of her eyes getting bigger and bigger until they looked like two flashlights in the dark.

We stood stone still for only a few seconds, but it seemed like an eternity until we heard the lieutenant walk away.

I let out a sigh of relief and Logan slowly crawled off the bed.

"Logan," I said, "You're the best friend I've ever had in the entire world, but I am not going to get busted for being with you in a dark room after lights-out. We'll finish this stuff later."

We were close. What was mine was hers, and what was hers was mine. While I was in prison I allowed people to lean on me, and share their problems and fears, but when I needed a shoulder to lean on there was really no one I could turn to—except Logan. I think it was because Logan was a strong person, and she was able to understand when I needed to be alone and when I needed a strong shoulder or sympathetic ear. When Lee Jr. died, Logan was there by my side. When Koquice had Britainny, Logan was there. When I suffered setbacks in the court system, Logan was there. She was always there with the right words whenever I needed them the most. She was the only inmate with whom I ever shared my deepest dreams and secrets. We call each other "Sis" because we are as close as two sisters can be.

Carla Hogue was another close friend. Carla can only be described as an arrogant, cocky white girl who, if she likes you, will do anything you ask and give you the shirt off her back if you need it. She is serving a fifty-year aggravated sentence for killing her common-law husband. Carla is the classic example of an abused woman ending up in prison for defending herself. The courts, for some reason, seldom recognize the extenuating circumstances involved when an abused woman is pushed to the brink of her endurance and strikes back in fear and anger. The prisons are filled with women serving hard time, convicted for killing the men who abused them.

Carla feels she killed her husband in self-defense. The jury disagreed, the courts denied her appeals, and she has almost sixteen more years to serve before becoming eligible for parole.

The experience has made her a bitter and extremely cynical woman. Yet towards me she was always as sweet as could be. More importantly, she was a good friend—someone I could depend on in any situation.

Gee Gee was another of the girls in our inner circle. She is doing time for a murder she says she didn't commit. She was convicted for killing her boyfriend, but she claims another woman did the crime. She will have served twenty years before becoming eligible for parole.

Despite the fact that Gee Gee is bitter, she is a very friendly, caring and giving person. And funny? This woman makes everyone laugh. She is a natural comedienne and a dancing fool. She is also a perfectionist. Gee Gee makes ends meet by knitting and crocheting things for other inmates. Buying something made by Gee Gee is a guarantee of perfection. It has to be exactly right or she will tear the stitches out and begin all over. I used to see her tear something apart a dozen times until she finally got a scarf or sweater exactly the way she wanted it.

Sometimes Gee Gee and I would talk for hours about our families and our cases. "I love my family, Joyce, and I know they love me, but I can't believe how your family has stuck by you all these years."

I'd nod. "The Lord's taking care of me, child. He gave me a family like that."

I don't think she was resentful of the fact that my family never wavered in their support, but there was a little envy there. Envy in that she felt if she had received that kind of support, she would not be facing such a long sentence and bleak future.

As I've mentioned, many inmates called me "Mama," "Granny," or "Auntie." I did not have, nor did I need, a mama, granny, or auntie. Logan was "Sis," but all other inmates were addressed by their names—with the exception of Ernestine. She was an elderly lady who always called me her "baby." For fun, I'd pretend I was mad and say something like, "Get away from here, girl. I ain't your baby and you ain't my mama. My mama lives in Dallas. I don't have any family in this place."

"No, that's not right," she'd say. "You're my baby, my only baby in here."

One day I was standing behind Ernestine in the commissary line and one of the inmates walked up, hugged her and said, "Hi, Mama." I could see her look to her left, look to her right, and when she didn't see me, she said to the inmate, "Hi, baby."

You know how you can stand behind someone and bend at your knees so your kneecaps kind of go into the other person's joints? That's what I did to Ernestine. She fell to the ground, rolled over, looked up, and saw me.

When we went back to the dorm, she kept telling everyone, "My baby pushed me to the ground today."

"You right, girl, but I'm not your baby. I pushed you to the ground because your other baby came around looking for her mama. I'm not going to be one of your many kids. I'm the only baby or I'm no baby at all."

"Oh, honey," she whined. "You know mama's getting old and I didn't hear that child call me mama. She's just some little old mixed-up kid. You're my only baby."

So I called her mama.

Ernestine was in prison for running scams, conning people out of their money. When she was in her early fifties, she ran one scam too many, got caught, and ended up in prison. Hoping to get her sentence reduced, she wrote to a lawyer someone had recommended. When she received his answer, Ernestine sat right down and wrote him another letter.

The lawyer had told her he would take on her case, but that first her family would have to pay him a retainer up front. Then they would have to do this, do that, get this, get that, and continue paying for his services. So she wrote, "If you think I'm going to let my family pay you all that money and then go out and do all the work they've paid you to do, you're crazy. I'm in prison for doing what you're trying to do to us!"

While it is possible to get along without friends, they certainly go a long way toward making life behind the walls more bearable This is especially true during the holidays when you need friends to make the best of the loneliest time of the year. One Christmas, I decided that our dorm needed a Christmas party. From the dayroom, I announced, "All right everybody, listen up. We're going to have a Christmas party and everybody is going to pitch in and help."

Most of the inmates came out and we began discussing plans to make the party one of the best ever. However, more than just a few remained in their cubicles as if they were not interested. These were the indigent inmates, those without money to give towards a party.

I went into each of their cubicles and explained that the party was going to be for everyone and everyone would contribute. Those who couldn't give money would serve on the clean-up committee, the decorating committee, or do whatever else needed to be done. Finally, we were all in the dayroom planning away.

And it was a great party. We made sure there was plenty of food, plenty of gifts, and lots of fun.

Joyce had been such a good friend to everyone in the dorm and had done so many things for every inmate, we decided the Christmas party would be a good time for all of us to show our appreciation. So we planned, without her knowing it, a special program.

After the party was underway and all the presents had been opened, I got everyone's attention and we made a big circle in the dayroom with Joyce in the center, sitting on a chair. We all sang "Merry Christmas" to her and then our big surprise—an inmate dressed as a messenger boy—arrived with a singing telegram for Joyce.

"He" stood right in front of Joyce and sang this little song. When the song was over, "he" opened "his" coat and out popped this huge black crocheted penis, right in front of Joyce's face.

Lord, if you could have seen the expression on her face. Her big eyes got bigger, her mouth flew opened, and she turned red with embarrassment. You have to understand that Joyce never participated in any of the dorm's sex talk, she never watched anything suggestive on TV, and was really very reserved when the subject of sex came up. She's kind of a prude where

sex is concerned, so when that big black dick popped
out of that coat she nearly died.

–Michelle Bonner
Inmate, Mountain View Unit

I will never forget that Christmas party. I was so embarrassed, but
I couldn't help but laugh. Tears were rolling out of my eyes and the
dorm loved it. It wasn't often they got the best of Joyce Ann Brown,
but that Christmas, they really got a "gotcha" on me.

Some of my friendships were the result of my simply being a
normal human being, trying to help someone. One day I was on the
yard when I heard a voice call out, "Joyce!" I looked around, but the
only person I saw was Faith.

She was a troubled child, angry at the system and determined to
rebel against all authority. She was always fighting and was always
ending up in segregation. She once spent two years in there alone.

And curse the law? She'd cuss the officers, even the warden, from
Amazing grace to a floating opportunity. For some reason, Faith
hated Madame Butterfly and did nothing to hide her feelings from
her. Madame Butterfly used to get up from her desk and say, "Well,
I guess I'll go down and get my nightly cursing out because I'm going
to be called a bitch, a whore, a mother-fucker."

Faith and I never had much to do with each other, so when I realized
she was calling me, I was surprised. She walked over. "May I ask you
a question?"

"Sure," I answered.

"It's personal."

I smiled. "If it's too personal I just won't answer it. What do you
want to know?"

"I've heard all about your case and I believe you're innocent. How
do you do your time the way you do it? I'm here because I did a crime.
I'm guilty of what I'm accused of, but I just can't handle these people.
They just drive me to the point of no return."

I tried to explain.

"Faith, the reason we do our time differently is that I fight them,
just like you. I'm fighting them now, fighting for my freedom, but I

fight in a different way than cussing or striking back. When you're fighting people in the professional world, you have to fight them in a whole new way. You can't fight them like you're in the streets.

"You're an inmate. They think you're a nothing. A dog. When you do what you do, you merely convince them that everything they've been told and taught is true. You're nothing but a dirty dog and you don't deserve to be treated like a human.

"Now, I don't love 'em. But I have a choice. I can either fight them like you and go to segregation, or I can do my job and when they do something I don't like or something I consider an insult, I can talk to them in an intelligent manner. Half the time they don't even know what I'm saying because they don't have the education I have.

"Half of them don't even have my common sense or street smarts, so I can play them out of pocket real quick and say things to them in such a way they think I'm being nice when actually I'm being downright nasty and rude."

I added one more thing. "And remember, God helps, too. Talk to him sometime."

A few days later, I was in the chapel on a Sunday morning. I was scheduled to sing the solo that morning and had selected a favorite hymn. As I looked across the room and saw Faith sitting there, I realized why I had chosen it.

I said, "I'm going to try to sing this song and I want to dedicate it to my new-found friend, Faith. We had a talk the other day and I told her I was in control of my life. But I lied to you, Faith, and I want to ask you to forgive me. When you listen to this song, you'll know that it's not me who is in control of my life, but God."

And I began to sing the old spiritual.

When the storms in my life are raging,
It's not easy.
When the weight of this world drives me to my knees,
I'm safe,
And I'm sure.
I feel so secure, you see,
I've found a hiding place,
And it's in God's love.

Yes, I'm leaning on Jesus,
Hallelujah!
He's the answer,

He's the only answer
To my every need.
He'll never leave me,
Never forsake
Or deceive me.
You see, I've found a hiding place
And it's in God's love.

I don't know if I helped Faith in her battle, but I do think I was able to help others cope with day-to-day life in prison—not only by counseling with them but by being an example as well. I know I was able to help Janice Holmes, an inmate in her late thirties who was serving a sixty-year sentence for aggravated robbery.

One day Janice received a message that reopened one of my old wounds. Her two sons had been playing with a rifle when it accidentally discharged, killing the older boy. As soon as I was able, I talked to Janice. Honestly and quietly, I explained what she could expect in regard to her emotions. I told her she had to let go. Sometimes she would have good days and sometimes bad days, but the important thing was that she not fight her emotions, not try to keep them bottled up inside. Her life would never be the same after receiving that message, and she needed to accept that.

Later a mutual friend of ours, Wilda, told me Janice had gone back to her dorm and told her, "Joyce is really sincere. She talked to me like she knew what I was going through."

Wilda said, "She does know what you're going through. Her stepson shot himself a few years ago, and she went through the same thing you're going through now."

Janice couldn't believe it. She had been in the unit with me all those years and had never heard about Lee's death.

I remembered the insensitivity of the prison officers who had refused to let me call home or attend the funeral. So first, I arranged for Janice to be allowed to meet with me anytime she needed to talk. Then, and more importantly, I used what little influence I had with a few of the officers to insure that she was able to telephone home regularly. This enabled her to have at least some measure of family love and support during that traumatic period.

After that time, I would occasionally see Janice and I began to notice that she was a stronger person. She took control of her life and was able to face what had happened with grace and strength. I like to think I played a small part in making her become more aware of her own strength. She learned to talk of her son in the past tense without breaking down, although I knew, like me, she was still hurting on the inside.

Then something wonderful happened.

On April 14, 1988, I received a letter from Kate Germond, Jim McCloskey's assistant at Centurion Ministries. Kate stated that they were getting ready to take on a Texas and Louisiana case, and since Jim would be coming to Texas, she wondered if I could forward a little more information on my case.

I raced to my stationary box, sat down, wrote her a letter, and mailed it off. Within two weeks, I received another letter in which Kate asked additional questions. Again, I didn't mess around. I had my answers in the return mail.

A month later, I received a third letter from Kate. As I read it, I could feel my heart begin to race. "Jim McCloskey will be visiting you in August for a personal interview."

At last, someone was taking an interest in Joyce Ann Brown.

12

The White Knights

As all lawyers and jurists know, but most lay people do not, innocence or guilt is irrelevant when seeking redress in the appellate courts.

As the noted attorney F. Lee Bailey observed, "Appellate courts have only one function, and that is to correct legal mistakes of a serious nature made by a judge at a lower level. Should a jury have erred by believing a lying witness, or by drawing on attractive but misleading inferences, there is nothing to appeal."

So, if the imprisoned innocent person is unable to persuade the appellate judges of any legal errors at trial, and generally he cannot, even though he suffered the ultimate trial error, he has no recourse. Nothing can be done legally to free him unless new evidence somehow surfaces that impeaches the validity of the conviction. Commonly, the incarcerated innocent are rubber-stamped into oblivion throughout the appeals process, both at the state and federal level.

*So where does that leave the innocent person once he
is convicted? Dead in the water, that's where! He is
screaming his head off that he is innocent, but no one
believes him.*

–James McCloskey, *Criminal Justice Ethics*
Winter/Spring 1989

A friend of mine refers to Jim McCloskey and Centurion Ministries as "the court of last resort." They jump right in there where no
one else will and battle for those who have been wrongly accused and
convicted.

Centurion Ministries derives its name from the Gospel of Luke,
23:47. A Roman soldier looks at Jesus and states, "Surely, this one
must be innocent." Their letterhead announces their goal: "Seeking
justice for the innocent in prison."

I couldn't believe that this organization had retained my original
letter in their files for nearly three years. That was a good sign. What
impressed me even more, however, was the story of Jim McCloskey
himself. Sitting in my cubicle, late at night, I read the materials Kate
Germond had sent me.

For years McCloskey had been a conservative Republican, living
in suburban Philadelphia and working as an international business
consultant. However, he was dissatisfied with his work and affluent
lifestyle. So much so that in 1979 he quit his job, abandoned the
business world, and entered Princeton Theological Seminary to
become a minister.

As part of his training, McCloskey, along with several other
seminary students, was assigned as student chaplain to the New
Jersey state prison in Trenton. Because he was older and more
experienced than his fellow students, Jim was assigned to the maximum security cells where the lifers were doing their time. It was there
he met, befriended, and became interested in George "Chiefie" De
Los Santos who was serving a life sentence for the 1975 murder of a
Newark used car salesman.

Jim like most people, was skeptical of any claim of innocence by
an inmate, but De Los Santos was so persistent and so steadfast in his
denial of guilt that Jim went home over the Thanksgiving holiday

determined to review the man's case. He spent the entire holiday vacation reading transcripts, studying police reports, and talking to people. By the time the holiday was over, Jim was convinced that De Los Santos was innocent. He committed himself to correcting the injustice.

Almost three years later, after an intensive effort, McCloskey proved beyond the shadow of a doubt that the prosecution's star witness—a jailhouse witness who had testified in exchange for leniency on a pending criminal charge—had committed perjury. In 1983, De Los Santos walked out of prison a free man.

Based on that experience, Jim McCloskey founded Centurion Ministries and dedicated himself to working in behalf of other inmates he felt were innocent. Within a few years he had obtained the releases of Rene Santana, in jail on a wrongful murder conviction; Milton Hernandes, wrongfully convicted for rape; and Nate Walker, who spent ten years behind bars for kidnapping and rape.

These four men were not released on a technicality or through some legal loop-hole, but as the result of solid new evidence uncovered by Jim McCloskey, evidence which proved conclusively that each man had been unjustly arrested and convicted.

And the miracle man was scheduled to visit with me.

On the morning of June 3, 1988, I got up early. I had prayed some heavy prayers during the night and, as might be expected, I was a nervous, nervous woman. This fear kept running through my head that I would go down, meet him, tell my story, and he would sympathize with me, say goodbye, and never contact me again.

Finally they called me down. I entered the visitor's room, sat down, looked through the chicken-wire and said, "Hello. I'm Joyce Brown."

A big smile broke out over that handsome man's face, and right that minute I knew God had sent me Jim McCloskey.

He looked like a New Yorker. I can always tell Yankees from Texas men. He was in his forties, partially baldheaded, and had an air of exuberant confidence that immediately relaxed me.

We chatted about this and that for a moment or two and then he got right down to business. "Joyce, I've read all your letters and newspaper clippings, but I need you to explain to me in your own words exactly what happened."

For the hundredth time, I began to tell my story. The whole time I was talking, he kept saying, "I can't believe that," or "Why do they do stuff like that?" Over and over again, he would say, "Incredible!" "Unbelievable!"

I had talked non-stop for about thirty minutes when he suddenly said, "Hold that thought a minute."

This sounded like the part where he would bow out of my life gracefully. But he went on, "Joyce, I'm going to do something I don't usually do. I'm going to commit to your case right here and now, because the more I talk to you the angrier I get."

I know my mouth dropped opened and I started to let out a squeal of joy, but I caught myself because I really couldn't believe I had heard right. "What did you say?"

He gave me that little grin of his and repeated, "I'm going to commit to you right this minute that I'm going to take on your case. There are at least a dozen other cases that I am looking into but they will have to wait until I get started on yours. What I usually do is talk to everyone first, then go back to New Jersey, review all the cases, and let the inmates know by letter what my decision is. But I can't do that to you. Something inside me tells me I have to take the case now."

I was shocked. Absolutely numb with joy. Afraid to wake up and find that it was all a dream.

"When I get back to my office, I'll write you a letter of confirmation, but for now, take it to the bank—I'm going to work on your case."

We continued talking for another two or three hours, and he advised me that the next time he came to visit, his private investigator would be with him. He also warned me that the process might take a long time. Centurion Ministries only takes on cases in which an inmate has a long sentence because their investigations involve such an extensive investment of time and effort. But he assured me, "Once we investigate your case there will be no doubt of your innocence, because we will have checked everything out."

All too fast, the visit ended. He left and I returned to my dorm. As I walked back, I felt such joy inside, but I didn't want to let that joy out. There was always a chance that something might happen or somebody might say something to change his mind before he sent the letter of confirmation. Even when I got back to the dorm and shared the news with Logan, Carla, and several other ladies, I kept my feelings bottled up. My friends were excited and began jumping around, laughing and joking as if I was scheduled to be released that day.

"Lawd, child, before you know, you'll be outta here and gone," Logan said.

Carla agreed. "You'll be writing us letters from the free world. Think of it. Free. Out in the world again."

I just smiled and tried to move the conversation onto other things.

For the next few days, I just went about my business, held my breath, waited, and waited, and waited until finally, the letter came.

> *Dear Joyce:*
>
> *This letter will confirm our conversation of June 3, 1988 in which I stated that Centurion Ministries agrees to accept you as a client. Be advised that, as quickly as possible, we will begin working on your case and will do everything within our means to prove that you have been unjustly accused and incarcerated. We will work to get you freed.*

Thank God! I could have jumped ten feet in the air. My prayers had been answered. The relief spread over my body and the joy finally came out.

Quickly I wrote a letter to Kerry to advise him of what was going on and to request that he provide Jim with anything he needed in his investigation. Then I wrote MaDear and told her the good news. That night, for the first time in years, I fell right to sleep.

That October Jim returned for a visit, and this time his private investigator, Richard Reyna, was with him. With his narrow waist and broad muscular shoulders, Richard must have been into bodybuilding. You could tell he was proud of the way he looked by the way he walked and talked. He had the look of a self-made man about him, and when I looked into his eyes I knew he wasn't afraid of anything. As Jim had done earlier, he made me feel comfortable.

Most of our visit was spent rehashing the events of my case. This time it was Richard who expressed disbelief that such flimsy evidence had held up in a court of law. I also told them all I knew about Martha Jean Bruce. Jim was especially interested in her story.

According to stories that inmates in the county jail had told me, back in 1980 representatives from the Dallas district attorney's office had visited the prison prior to my trial. They requested interviews with every woman who had been in the Dallas county jail with me while I was waiting to make bond. At the time, Martha Jean was serving a five-year sentence in the Texas women's prison at Mountain View for attempted murder.

One can only guess what must have transpired during Martha's interview, but at my trial Kerry had raised questions about the validity of her testimony. The transcript reads:

Fitzgerald: "They [the prosecutors] didn't encourage you to talk to them by promising you a thing?"
Bruce: "They didn't promise me nothing."
Fitzgerald: "You don't expect any kind of a time cut?"
Bruce: "No."
Fitzgerald: "Have you asked the district attorney's office to write a letter to the Board of Pardons and Paroles recommending early parole?"
Bruce: "No."
Fitzgerald: "Do you expect them to do that?"
Bruce: "No."

Yet one month after my trial, then-District Attorney Henry Wade wrote a letter to the Texas Board of Pardons and Paroles asking that Martha Jean's five-year sentence be reduced to two years. In his letter, Mr. Wade said:

> *Certain facts unknown to the state and the court at the time Mrs. Bruce was convicted of attempted murder have come to our attention. It now appears that immediately prior to the time Mrs. Bruce shot and wounded the complainant, he, the complainant, had threatened Mrs. Bruce with a knife. The mitigating circumstances surrounding her conviction were not considered in assessing her punishment, and we now believe the sentence of five years is excessive.*

Within a few weeks of receiving Mr. Wade's letter, the parole board recommended to the governor that Bruce's sentence be commuted. On December 30, 1980, just three months after I was convicted by her testimony, Governor Bill Clements signed the order and on July 30, 1981, Martha Jean Bruce was released from prison. She had served fourteen months of her five-year sentence.

Jim was very excited about that information and thought it would be enough to get me released, but as I explained to him, Kerry had already filed a writ back in 1984 based on the suspicious nature of those events. The appeal was denied. "This is Texas. That's not enough. More is needed to get the Appeals Court to grant a new trial."

Then we moved on to the future. Jim told me about an arrangement he had made with the Mountain View Unit warden for a monthly telephone call. This would enable him to fill me in on the progress of the investigation, and I could continue to provide names of family, friends, and others who might be able to assist him and Richard. Richard surprised me with the news that they had obtained permission to visit with Rene Taylor.

Finally our visit was over and they prepared to go see Rene. I warned them, "She hasn't been too cooperative before."

Richard smiled and said, "She's never talked to Jim before either. He's got a way of making people open up."

As I rose to leave, Richard had one more piece of news for me. "You're married, kiddo, to Jim and me. And we won't divorce you until we get you out of this place."

It was a good feeling. All of the sudden I had five white men working in my behalf. Along with Jim and Richard there was, of course, Kerry, my faithful Rock of Gibraltar. Since the very beginning, his faith never wavered. He stuck by me year in and year out, never receiving a dime for his efforts to turn around my conviction.

There was also Steve McGonigle, a reporter for *The Dallas Morning News*. He had grown interested in my case as early as 1984 and arranged for an interview with me at Mountain View. After we talked for nearly four hours he returned to Dallas convinced, as he later told Kerry, that "Joyce Ann Brown is an innocent woman." Since that time, Steve had used every available opportunity to write an article favorable to me. He was the only Dallas media person who persistently raised questions concerning the validity of my trial.

Steve McGonigle had recently interested another influential reporter in my case, Steve Blow. Both of them were now working to get stories about me into the *The Dallas Morning News* whenever they could.

My white knights were restoring color to my life, and when I think of them I am reminded of the time Jesus spoke about "fishers of men." Each time God brought someone into my life, that person would bring someone else. It was like a schedule was being kept.

In February, 1989, Jim and Richard visited me again. As we sat down, Jim said, "We've uncovered something important to your case." I listened quietly as the two explained what they had uncovered.

Armed with the information I had provided them about Martha Jean Bruce and with additional documents from Kerry, Jim and Richard had focused their initial investigation on the woman who had played such a major role in my conviction. In an interview, Martha Jean Bruce had admitted to Jim that she had lied; but the admission was not taped and she later recanted. Jim and Richard turned back to the trial transcripts.

When Dallas prosecutor Norman Kinne had called Martha Jean Bruce to the stand, he had asked her to recite her criminal history, which included theft, burglary, and attempted murder. He had also provided Kerry with her rap sheet. Under cross-examination, Kerry had asked Martha whether she had any convictions other than those on her rap sheet or those she had revealed under Norman Kinne's questioning. Under oath, she replied she did not.

Jim and Richard discovered otherwise.

On July 15, 1979, Martha Jean was arrested for telling two policemen that she had been robbed of $180, when in fact she had actually stolen the money herself and had hidden it in her south Dallas apartment. Jim and Richard found Dallas County court records dated March 13, 1980, which indicated that Martha Jean Bruce pleaded guilty to a charge of making a false statement to a peace officer. For that, she was sentenced to ten days in the county jail.

In other words, when Martha Jean Bruce took the stand at my trial, she was already a *convicted liar*. And Jim and Richard were just getting warmed up.

They always kept careful notes on all research and interviews, including their first meeting with Rene Taylor on the day Jim brought Richard to meet me. In that meeting, she had made a comment in passing that she and "Delores" could not go back to Albuquerque. However, an attempt to persuade her to identify "Delores" failed. Nor would she explain about "Albuquerque."

Jim decided to concentrate on the mysterious "Delores" and her Albuquerque connection to Rene. In a second interview with Rene, she again refused to tell who helped her rob the Dallas fur store and would not identify "Delores." However, she did tell them, "Find the woman who was in Albuquerque with me and you'll find my accomplice in the Dallas robbery."

Albuquerque ? No one had ever mentioned a robbery in Albuquerque. Richard and Jim began checking.

They found that at the time Rene Taylor was being hunted by Dallas police (and the FBI) for her participation in the robbery of Fine Furs by Rubin, she was under indictment in Albuquerque for the 1978 robbery of Lloyd's Furriers. More importantly, another woman had also been indicted for that crime. That woman, Lorraine Germany, had been acquitted in a jury trial but was serving a sixteen-year prison sentence in the Colorado state prison at Canon City for yet another crime—the armed robbery of a fast food store.

The Albuquerque and Dallas furrier robberies proved to have a lot in common. In each, both robbers were black women wearing jogging suits, one woman carried a pistol while shouting orders to the store employees, and the furs were stuffed into black plastic garbage bags.

But that wasn't all. Jim had visited Colorado to interview Lorraine Germany. "Joyce," he said, leaning in close to the plexiglass window between us, "when she walked into that visiting room, I nearly fell off my chair. She looked enough like you to be your twin sister."

It was about this time, in January, 1989, that Jim and Richard dropped another bombshell into the lap of the Dallas district attorney. Both were intrigued by the fact that when Rene Taylor was convicted for her participation in the Dallas furrier robbery, the decision to plea bargain her charge rather than face a jury trial was obviously motivated by the fact that not only had she been identified as one of the robbers, but that her fingerprints had been found on hangers taken from the fur store as well.

Jim and Richard wondered if any other fingerprints had been lifted from the hangers found in the getaway car. And, if so, were they still available in the evidence property room of the Dallas police department?

Bingo! Unidentified fingerprints did indeed exist in the police files. Jim guessed, correctly, that when the police were unable to match my fingerprints with those on the hangers they had made no further effort to determine who else's prints they might be. He suggested publicly, on television and in the newspapers, that if the police and district attorneys analyzed the unidentified prints, they might be able to match them with the fingerprints of Lorraine Germany.

Interestingly, Detective Tommy Barnes, who investigated the Dallas robbery, and First Assistant District Attorney Norman Kinne, who prosecuted it, both said they remembered that a fingerprint belonging to Rene Taylor was found on a coat hanger, but they did not recall any unidentified prints. I remembered learning at my trial that there was only one fingerprint found in the entire getaway car. Eight years later Jim had found four more, and on March 11, 1989, *The Dallas Morning News* reported that Lorraine Germany's fingerprints were compared to 25 sets of prints. To this day, I wonder where all those fingerprints were during my trial.

All of a sudden, the Dallas media rediscovered my case. Steve Blow and Steve McGonigle began writing about my case, and I soon was being featured in every newspaper and on every television station in Dallas. Writers and newscasters were raising the subject of my innocence. They suggested that the fingerprints could lead to a reversal in my case.

I don't know what I expected. Perhaps I thought that the courts would immediately jump into the case. But of course, our legal system doesn't work that way. Evidence must be concrete and unquestionable. Even then, as I kept learning, the wheels of justice move ever so slowly and methodically. The district attorney's office took its time before even responding to the questions raised by the media.

However, enough public pressure was generated to force the Dallas police to transmit the prints to Colorado authorities with a request that they compare them to those of Lorraine Germany. Within a few days, word was received from Colorado: a comparison of the prints was inconclusive. McCloskey contacted the district attorney's office and requested that another comparison be made. Somehow, he was able to convince them to accept his request and another set of prints was mailed to Colorado to be compared with those of Lorraine Germany.

While the fingerprints were being forwarded, Norman Kinne publicly declared the comparison carried little significance.

Steve McGonigle, in the March 2, 1989 edition of the *Morning News*, wrote:

> But even if Lorraine Germany's fingerprints match the Dallas evidence, Kinne said, that will not convince him of Ms. Germany's involvment in the robbery or the innocence of a Dallas woman convicted in the crime. "It's not evidence of anything other than at some time she handled some coat hangers. That's not an offense," Kinne said.

Then, the bad news. The results were received from Colorado, and Kinne announced to the press that the fingerprints found in the getaway car failed to match those of Lorraine Germany. "It tells me Lorraine Germany was not involved and was not even in Dallas as far as I can tell." He added that the results concluded his inquiry into my conviction.

Although Kinne's comments shattered my hopes, I had received a new lease on life as a result of all the local publicity. For the first time, the national media became interested in my case.

Soon after Kinne's announcement, I received word from the Count Office that I had a long distance call from a television reporter. I went into the office and spoke to a representative from *Inside Edition* who requested an interview. I agreed and a young gentleman by the name of Scott Rappaport came to Mountain View to conduct the interview.

I had been on local television many times, but this was my first experience with a national program. Once again, I went through the details of my arrest and conviction. I greatly appreciated the publicity, but I will never forget the man who conducted the interview.

When we finished taping the interview and the camera had been turned off, Mr. Rappaport leaned in close and asked, "Just between you and me, off the record, did you do it?"

I had to bite my tongue before I answered. But when I did, I said as sweetly as possible—and with a smile, "No, I didn't do it." The young hotshot should be thankful for the sheet of chicken-wired plexiglass that separated us at that moment.

Several days later, the program was aired and I was able to watch it on the dorm television. As might be expected, I received a lot of ribbing, but I was pleased. My message was getting out beyond the state of Texas. Now the rest of the country would discover what was going on in our justice system.

Shortly after the program aired, MaDear came to visit. She was excited about seeing her daughter on a national television program and, for most of the visit, we talked about how many people had been calling her to report they had also seen it. Before she left, she casually mentioned, "By the way, the man responsible for getting your program aired called me."

"Oh." I had assumed one of the local television stations had arranged for the interview or even that Jim McCloskey had somehow been involved. MaDear went on. "Yes, a writer in Dallas by the name of Jay Gaines. I have his address if you want to write him."

Well, I certainly wanted to write and thank him, and I did. That letter put together a final piece of the puzzle which would eventually set me free. Little did I realize how close I was to reaching my goal: Freedom!

13

Things Begin To Happen

Joyce Ann Brown greeted us in the prison visiting room, smiling and gracious, as if we were guests in her home.

"It's nice to meet you," she said to me, nodding from behind the glass and wire screen that separated us.

"And it's good to see you again," she said, turning to my colleague, Steve McGonigle, who had visited her five years ago in this same prison.

The folded tissue in her hand was the only clue that rough going lay ahead.

In a sense, this drab visiting room in the Mountain View prison unit north of Gatesville is the closest thing Joyce has to a home. For the last nine years, she has greeted her family here every other weekend.

"I put on a front for them. I smile and tell them that everything is fine," she said, fighting the quaver rising in her voice.

*But of course everything is not fine. She is in prison.
And she is in prison for a crime she swears she did
not commit.*

*The Joyce Ann Brown case has bothered many for a
long time. Over the years public interest in the case
has come and gone. Now it has come again.*

*"Yes," she said, "It gets tiresome discussing my case
again and again, but this is my freedom I'm talking
about, so regardless of how tired I get, I have to keep
on talking."*

*I feel sorry for Mrs. Danziger and all that has hap-
pened to her. But I also feel sorry for Joyce Brown.
She's a victim, too."*

She has but one solace.

*"I'm here in this prison doing the time. I'm hurt.
Sometimes I'm disgusted. But the one thing I'm not is
guilty. I'm not guilty. I can lie down at night and sleep
free."*

–Steve Blow, *The Dallas Morning News*
March 20, 1989

Shortly after Steve Blow's column ran, *The Dallas Morning News*
published a very important article concerning yet another avenue of
hope. Steve McGonigle had written a story. When I saw the headline
of the March 26 issue, my heart stopped. "JURY WASN'T TOLD
WITNESS LIED TO POLICE. OMISSION MAY HELP BROWN
GET A NEW TRIAL."

McGonigle had interviewed several jurors from my trial and one,
Charles H. Miller, said he would not have voted to convict me if he
had known the full story behind Martha Jean Bruce's testimony. "It

would have brought up a little more doubt in my mind and I know it wouldn't have taken but a little to get me to vote not guilty."

In fact, according to the story, four of the jurors had initially voted to acquit me in the trial but changed their votes after comparing testimony between Mrs. Danziger, Martha Jean, and me. From the D.A.'s point of view, it was easy to see what an advantage it was to have a jailhouse witness at one's disposal who was willing to perjure herself.

It was now a point of public record that my conviction had resulted from the testimony of a woman with a reputation for lying. In my heart, I could not see how they could keep me in jail any longer. But in my mind, I knew they could. And they did.

April arrived, then May, and I was still going about my daily routine: eating, sleeping, working, and waiting. Jim kept my spirits up by continuing to assure me that it was only a matter of time. Kerry was hopeful about a writ he was preparing to file that summer which requested a new trial. He was also glad to have another attorney working on my behalf.

The demands of the case had reached a point where it was just too much for one attorney, so Kerry had gone out looking for help. After approaching several interested lawyers, Kerry settled on Jack Strickland.

As a former prosecutor, Jack's working style is aggressive, impetuous, while Kerry tends to be more methodical, conservative, even subdued. However, his quiet demeanor masks the competitive spirit that makes him such a good lawyer. His quiet strength was complimented by Jack's rapid-fire energy, and each concentrated on his own strengths to move my case along quickly.

Kerry was very uncomfortable with all the media attention. I don't know why—he's handsome, personable, and handles himself better than most politicians. But cameras and interviewers just make him nervous. If he had his way Kerry would avoid them altogether, but at this point there was no alternative—he was being hounded from every angle, at his office and at home.

Jack is also a good-looking man. A prematurely grey head of hair gives him a distinguished look and, unlike Kerry, he thoroughly enjoys meeting and bantering with the media.

Kerry was also glad to have a "foreigner"—an out-of-town attorney—battling beside him in what might turn out to be an all-out war against a Dallas judge and the Dallas D.A. Jack's office was in Fort Worth—far enough away to be an advantage but only a short drive from Dallas—so he was readily available for conferences with Kerry and me or for any hearing. I considered myself extremely lucky to have two such attorneys in my corner.

And yet another white knight came into my life that summer. I had finally made contact with Jay Gaines.

When I mailed him a short thank-you note for his efforts in getting *Inside Edition* interested in my story, I didn't expect to hear from him again. But I did and in his return letter, Jay said he might be able to interest several magazines in running an article on me. He requested me to sit down and, in my own words, tell him what had happened.

So many times over the years, I had complied with similar requests for information, only to see the stories come to nothing. I never refused a single request: It might come to nothing, but it was another chance to keep my case before the public. So late one night I sat down and scribbled off three or four pages describing the circumstances of my imprisonment. Next morning, I dropped the thing in the mail and forgot about it.

Several weeks later Jay responded.

His letter spoke of how he had been "moved to tears, to anger, to frustration" each time he read my letter. He wanted to become actively involved in the case, promising to do everything in his power to bring it to the attention of everyone remotely capable of righting this wrong.

I think what impressed me about his letter were his comments after listing several ideas for raising general awareness of my case. He said that the list was not meant "to create another *era* or *sense* of false hope for you. These are simply things that can be done. Whether they will accomplish anything remains to be seen. At least, you will know someone else is working in your behalf." Jay proposed to write several magazine articles about me, initiate letter campaigns to Texas authorities and newspapers, and utilize his contacts in the television industry to obtain more national coverage.

On July 30, I received a copy of a letter Jay had mailed to Patti Hassler, a producer of *60 Minutes*. In the letter he outlined a list of individuals and publications supporting my claim of innocence and proposed that my story be used as the subject for a *60 Minutes* segment. He also slipped in a note advising me not to grant any interviews with any national television program while *60 Minutes* was considering his request. Their program would obviously have more impact than any other, and if I showed up on a competitor's program, I might be dropped from consideration.

I couldn't help but shake my head at his sweet note. In addition to my failure to interest the news program back in 1985, Jim McCloskey had tried again, without success, just last year. But I sat down and wrote a polite thank-you to Jay for his efforts.

A few days later, Kerry and Jack filed another writ in my behalf requesting a new trial. The writ alleged that prosecutors had suppressed critical evidence and presented perjured testimony during the 1980 trial. It also stated that prosecutor Norman Kinne had improperly withheld information about a similar robbery in 1978 in Albuquerque, New Mexico. It contended that Kinne had improperly withheld the record of Martha Jean Bruce which showed she had once been convicted of lying.

The writ maintained that my conviction was "the direct result of the illegal, unprofessional, and unethical conduct" of Norman Kinne. It contended that had Kinne made a complete disclosure, the jury that convicted me would have reached a different decision about my guilt in this case.

As part of the request, Kerry filed affidavits from two jurors stating that they would not have voted to convict me had they known about Martha Jean Bruce's prior conviction for lying. In the affidavits, both jurors also asked that I be granted a new trial.

I had learned not to get my hopes up, but this time they were being bolstered by press coverage of the events. Within three days of the filing of my appeal another juror from my trial publicly expressed doubts about the outcome of my trial. Mr. Dan Peeler, in an interview with Steve Blow, said he had been plagued with uncertainty about my conviction for years. Based on what he had learned from news stories, he had changed his opinion and said, " I don't think she's guilty . . . .She's got to have a new trial."

To back up his words, he provided Kerry with a handwritten statement, also filed with the court, in which he wrote: "I am now convinced we have sent an innocent woman to prison, and I am willing to do whatever is necessary and possible to help her regain her freedom."

My court hearing was set for October 23. The news was plastered all over the local media. Then, on August 23, I was summoned to the Count Office for a phone call. A woman representing *A Current Affair* told me they wanted to feature my story on their program and asked for permission to come down to Mountain View for an interview.

I was riding high. I accepted immediately, and we planned to talk again the following week to schedule an interview. But remembering Jay's hopeful note, I sat down and wrote to inform him of my plans. I knew they had already received permission from Kerry and had talked to Jim McCloskey, so I felt I was making the best decision.

The minute Jay received my letter, he hit the panic button. He called the prison, managed to get through to my Corrections Counselor and told her to get a message to me not to grant an interview to *A Current Affair*. He then contacted both Kerry and Jim and cautioned them against granting permission to any news program until *60 Minutes* had finalized their decision.

I had no way of knowing that when Jay learned of the new writ and the statements provided by the jurors in my trial, he had contacted Patti Hassler of *60 Minutes*. When he made her aware of the new developments, she voiced immediate interest and requested more information. Jay called Kerry and had him ship CBS News a copy of the new writ. Within just a few days, Jay was told that Morley Safer had become especially interested in my case and that Allen Weisman would be the producer of the segment. Next month, *60 Minutes* was coming to Mountain View.

On the morning of September 20, I was up at six to get ready for the interview, which was scheduled for one o'clock that afternoon. As usual, my "children" jumped in to help. I had my hair done, my nails manicured, and my skirt and blouse ironed to perfection.

I had seven hours to get ready for the interview, and I still wasn't ready. When they called me to come down, I was still gathering materials I thought I might need. I was running around like a chicken with its head cut off. Logan yelled out, "Joyce, you'll be late for your own funeral!"

Maybe. They were calling for me and I was yelling, "Wait! Wait, wait, wait. . . let me get this, I need that. . .wait wait, wait."

Finally, they pushed me out the door and I headed for the Count Office to pick up my escort to the visiting room. Instead of the usual guard or junior officer, I found myself accompanied by a guard, a captain, and the Fire and Safety officer. As we walked down, the Fire and Safety officer said, "Joyce, there is a slight hitch. You won't be able to use the contact visiting room."

For the first time that day, I got mad. We had a brand new visiting room, freshly painted and cleaned, but I was going to have to conduct an interview through the old familiar plexiglass and chickenwire. "Why's that?"

"For security," she answered.

No arguing with that. So I shrugged my shoulders, put on my smile, lifted my head in the air, and walked into the visiting room. There I sat down, looked through the chickenwire, and said, "Hello, I'm Joyce Brown."

A kind face smiled back. "Hello, I'm Morley Safer."

Without a doubt, it was the most relaxed and enjoyable interview I'd ever had. He was so easy to talk to. We talked about what had happened, how it felt to be innocent and in prison, and what my plans were.

When the interview was finished and I was getting ready to leave, one of the young ladies on the camera crew came up and said, "Ms. Brown, I just want you to know that I admire you. I admire your character and strength and how you've been fighting and struggling all these years."

I was so touched. Here was this stranger from New York, who surely had seen worse things in her career, saying such sweet things. In the background, I could hear the others saying, "Great. She was just great." I turned to Mr. Safer and he smiled. "Good-bye, Joyce, and good luck."

A week later, I was on my way to the administration building to wait for my monthly call from Jim, when a sergeant who was being transferred soon walked up and said, "Joyce, I very seldom get involved in an inmate's business, but I really hope for the best for you and wish you well."

We talked for a few minutes and then we were joined by another officer. Finally I said, "I have to get inside. I'll see you people later."

I went in, sat down, and another officer walked up and said, "Joyce, I wish you well on your bench warrant."

"Thank you, but I'm not leaving until next month."

She shook her head. "No, you're leaving today."

"Today?" I stood up. "My court date isn't until October twenty-third!"

She looked at me curiously and asked, "Didn't the sergeant tell you to get packed?"

"All he said to me was that he wished me good luck. He didn't say anything about getting packed."

"Girl, they called and said for you to be ready to leave at 11:00 this morning."

"I need to talk to my lawyer. It's too early for me to leave."

When I got Kerry on the phone, he verified that I was due back in Dallas that day and said he would explain everything when I got into town.

I passed word for someone to contact Logan so she could maneuver her way back to the dorm to help me get ready. By the time I left the administration building, the entire unit knew I was headed for Dallas. While Logan packed and I dressed, we tried to figure out why I was going back early. All Kerry had said was that the district attorney would be there. I knew that the D.A.'s office had lost my records, so maybe the hearing had something to do with forcing them to find my files.

Logan persuaded me to go down to the dining hall for lunch, reminding me that in Dallas all I would get would be a bologna sandwich, so she, Margaret and I went to eat. When we arrived there was a line a mile long, but when the other inmates saw us the line parted like the Red Sea. We walked right to the front of the line with everyone, inmates and officers, wishing me the best of luck.

By the time we finished eating, my name was called and I reported to the Count Office. Within a matter of minutes, I was in a car headed for Dallas.

First I was checked into the Lew Starret Jail and then transferred to the Government Center. Before I had even settled in, I called Jay. He hooked up his conference call and got MaDear on the line (her phone could not accept collect calls). After I talked to her, he called Kerry so we could find out what was going on.

Kerry was vague, but we kept badgering him until he said, "Joyce, I can't tell you what is going to happen tomorrow because I'm not really sure. But I think I can tell you that tomorrow might be the biggest day in your life."

On that cryptic note, we hung up. I slept very little that night.

The next morning, I was transferred to the holding room in Judge Chapman's court. There, Jack and Kerry sat down with me and Kerry tried to explain the writ in his hands. Finally I took the writ, read it myself, turned to Jack and asked, "Does this mean what I think it means?"

Jack laughed and said, "Yes."

Kerry could read someone the Pledge of Allegiance, as Jack used to say, and by the time he finished no one would understand what he was talking about. That's just the way Kerry is. He's a scholarly man.

But he gave it another shot. The district attorney had signed an affidavit agreeing that I had not received a fair trial in 1980. Armed with that affidavit, Kerry was going to present my writ to the court right then instead of waiting for the October 23 hearing. Ironically, the date was September 29th—the same date I had begun my trial nine years earlier.

The hearing took less than fifteen minutes. Judge Ron Chapman, the very judge who had first heard my case in 1980, presided. The D.A. stated that I had been sentenced without receiving a fair trial because prosecutors failed to disclose evidence key to the defense.

As I had learned in my 1984 appeal, the presiding judge always has the option of making or not making a recommendation to the Court of Appeals. It goes without saying that an appeal with a recommendation has a much stronger chance for a favorable review than one without.

After Kerry and the D.A. presented their joint request, Judge Chapman ruled. He accepted all statements and concluded that he would recommend to the Texas Court of Criminal Appeals that I be granted a new trial.

I buried my head in my arms on the table. I was afraid to breathe.

Based on the fact that both the judge and the district attorney agreed I had not received a fair trial and that I should have a new one, Kerry requested that I be allowed out on bond until the court ruled on my case. He suggested a $25,000 personal recognizance bond, pointing out to Judge Chapman that I had never failed to meet a bond or court appearance while waiting for my first trial. But the district attorney objected, so Judge Chapman had no choice but to refuse the request. He did, however, state that he would recommend to the Court of Appeals that I be granted bond while they reviewed my appeal.

They quickly escorted me from the courtroom to a small adjacent chamber where reporters were allowed in to interview me.

It was a difficult session. The impact of what had happened was only beginning to sink in. My family was only a few feet away, yet I couldn't talk to them, couldn't hold them, couldn't share my joy with them. Mercifully, the interviews soon ended and I was taken back to my jail cell in the Government Center.

I knew that on Monday morning, Kerry and Jack were flying to Austin to appeal directly to the Court for my bond, so I found myself spending a long weekend in that filthy, noisy jail. Instead of a bunk, I was handed a mattress and told to find a spot on the floor. But my good fortune was holding out.

Little Shawana was back in Dallas on a bench warrant to have her time reduced. Without a moment's hesitation, she said, "Granny, take my bed."

But I didn't want Shawana to sleep on the floor either, so I told her we would share. She could sleep stretched out from the foot and I would stretch out from the head. It was better than either of us sleeping on the floor.

That night I was awakened out of a deep sleep by a guard's voice. "Well, what do we have here?"

"What does it look like?" I stared her right back in the face. "We're sleeping. I'm not a homosexual and this is a child sleeping on this bed. If you want to write it up, just write it up. We're not moving."

She gave me a hard look and said, "You're Joyce Brown, aren't you?"

"Yes I am and I'm not hitting the floor. We'll be sleeping like this until I get a bed."

She went on about her business.

I couldn't have visitors because I had been back only one day—not long enough to get anyone's name on the visitors' list. But I could make phone calls, and thanks to Jay's three-way phone line I was able to spend almost the entire weekend on the telephone, talking to family, relatives, friends, and even reporters who called Jay to get to me.

Monday morning, Kerry and Jack flew to Austin, hand-carrying the request for bond in hopes that the court would rule immediately. Although the higher court usually refused bond, Kerry and Jack hoped it would make an exception because even the prosecutors agreed I had been unjustly convicted.

Bond was denied. The Court would not even consider the request until it had decided whether to grant me a new trial.

I was disappointed but not really surprised. I told everybody, including myself, that I had not expected the Court of Appeals to rule favorably on the bond issue because it had never been done before. It was hardest on MaDear. When she was told my bond request had been refused, she began screaming and crying, and then fainted. It scared everyone to death. But when she regained consciousness, she was her old strong self again and geared up her strength to wait on the Court's next decision.

With bond denied, I had the option of remaining in the Dallas county jail, where I could at least talk to my family every day on the telephone and receive visits from them every week, or I could return to Mountain View until a decision was made.

My decision may sound strange unless you've ever been inside the Dallas county jail. The tanks are so bad I could never get any sleep, so crowded I couldn't find a moment of privacy, and so filthy I could barely breathe. In addition, our worn-out jump suits and dingy sheets were changed only once a week, and the food had not improved since my last visit, either. I elected to return to Mountain View.

On the morning of October 9, I walked back into my old "home." As usual, nothing seemed to go as planned. When I left Dallas, Lew Starret officials would not let me keep anything I had arrived with. MaDear had to go down and sign for my possessions at the jail, where she learned that the officials had managed to lose something so dear to me that I could have started a riot—my college class ring, a beautiful ring that my sister Mary had given me when I got my degree.

I fired off a letter to Jay, told him the problem, and asked for his help. Speed was essential because the jail property room only allows you ten days to retrieve possessions; anything not picked up by then is removed.

Jay got the runaround for a bit but he kept calling and calling, each time going another step up the ladder of authority until finally, someone found my ring and MaDear was able to get it back to me. I looked upon its return as a sign that my luck was truly changing. And it was.

When Morley Safer interviewed me, he had said that the program would probably be broadcast the first week in October. For two Sundays in a row, everyone throughout the prison gathered around the television set and waited in vain for a sign of Joyce Ann Brown. I kept praying, "Lord, don't let anything happen anywhere that is more important than my story." Finally I received a letter from Jay. He had contacted New York and was told my segment was scheduled to run the following week, on Sunday, October 22. By six that evening, I was so nervous I could not sit still, but from the moment that familiar tick-tick-tick-tick began to sound, my nervousness just faded away. I drew a deep breath and listened to Morley Safer tell my story.

> *"The last time we did a story in Dallas about someone who may have been wrongly convicted of a crime, his name was Lenell Geter. When we caught up with him, he was in jail for life. Now we may have found another Lenell Geter, a woman. Her name is Joyce Ann Brown and when we caught up with her, she was also serving a life sentence, prosecuted by the same district attorney's office that put Geter away..."*

The Texas Court of Criminal Appeals is notoriously conservative and slow. I had been corresponding with Clarence Brandley, a death row inmate whose case had also been investigated by Jim Mc-Closkey. Clarence had been waiting for almost two years on an appeal decision from the Texas Court of Appeals. I knew my review could drag on that long, but Kerry and Jack were hoping for a decision sometime after Christmas.

Then, on the morning of November 1, I was awakened with a request to go see Ms. Powell in the Count Office office immediately. I was a little irritated at having my sleep disturbed, but also concerned that something might be wrong at home. When I walked in, Ms. Powell handed me the telephone receiver without a word.

It was Jay. "Are you sitting down, kid?"

"Yes," I answered, my heart pounding. He took a deep breath and then, in that beautiful golden voice of his, said, "Joyce Ann, the Texas Court of Criminal Appeals handed down their decision this morning. You're going to get a new trial."

I didn't scream out. I didn't squeal. I didn't go jumping around the room with joy. But I felt all those things. I just closed my eyes and whispered, "Praise God." Then I hesitated, "Are you absolutely sure?"

"I talked with one of the law clerks at the court. It's all over the news around here. You're being released on bond."

"When?"

"I can't answer that. I'll try to catch up with Kerry and see if he can find out. And as soon as I know, I'll call the warden and ask her to get word to you."

"Have you told my mama yet?"

"No, I wanted to tell you first."

I urged him to call her and Koquice, and then I had to hang up the phone. I wasn't even supposed to be using the telephone, but Ms. Powell bent the rules a little when she heard why Jay was calling.

The prison grapevine had already gone to work. Before I could leave Ms. Powell's office, inmates and officers began to gather at the door. Everyone knew it. I was going home.

14

Thanksgiving

The entire unit, without exception, was on an emotional high.

Out of all the years of my incarceration never before have I witnessed such anticipation, such joy, and such love as the officers and inmates displayed when it was learned that Joyce Brown was going home.

As the word began to race across the unit, inmates managed to work their way around to where Joyce was. Even the warden found time to come down and congratulate Joyce.

Just to have known her was, for everyone, something unique. I think I speak for everyone who knew her when I say that she touched us all in a very special way and we are each a better person for having known and loved Joyce Ann Brown.

–Joyce Logan
Inmate, Mountain View Unit

To say I was confused is an understatement. I had no idea what was going on. Newspapers were reporting that I would be released the following week. Television stations were saying it would take up to fifteen days to process and return me to Dallas. Jay called the Sheriff's office and was told that I could not return to Dallas any earlier than the following Monday because no deputies were available. Kerry, meanwhile, called to tell me he was doing everything in his power to get me released before the weekend.

True to his word, he applied enough pressure in the proper circles. A bench warrant was issued by a local judge ordering the Sheriff's Department to pick me up and return me to Dallas by no later than Friday, November 3. The Sheriff's office instructed the prison to have Inmate No. 198-507 ready for transfer at 10:00 a.m. on Friday.

It was official.

It is hard to imagine that a prison inmate would have much to pack, but after nine years, I had plenty. And I had no intention of following the prison rules which forbid a departing inmate from giving anything to other inmates. Other than a few personal items and my legal materials, I gave away everything—toiletries, commissary food, a radio, a typewriter, even my fourteen pairs of shoes.

That's right! Fourteen pairs of shoes. It might sound ridiculous, but I would have owned twice that many if I could get them. I saw absolutely no reason to sacrifice my appearance in prison. We may have had to wear prison whites, but we were allowed scarves or bandannas. Every day, my shoes matched whatever scarf I had chosen to dress up my uniform. Even in prison, I was fashion conscious.

On Friday, I woke up around six. I should say "got up" because I never really fell asleep. I was too nervous, too excited. As soon as I started moving around, women began stopping by the dorm on one excuse or another, all with the same purpose—to wish me well.

I didn't bother going to the dining hall for breakfast because I couldn't eat. Instead, Logan and Carla took me on a last walk around the unit. We would stop, visit with someone, and then continue on. Finally I said goodbye to Carla, Margaret, Joni, Ernestine, Michelle, Shirley—all who had become such close friends. To each and every one of them I promised to stay in touch by letter and by visiting.

It was a time of joy but also a time of sadness. I was so happy to be heading home to my family, but I was leaving another family behind. I would miss these ladies and many of the officers.

It was 11:00. The deputies from Dallas were an hour late. And then I got a call to report to Assistant Warden Cherry's office. My heart stopped. Walking into her office I feared the worst. "Joyce," she said, "I just wanted to tell you good-bye and wish you the best of luck."

There was a pause, and I waited for the bomb to drop. There's a slight hitch. There's been a change in plans. But she finished, "It has been a pleasure to know you and to work with you."

I thanked her, but had to know, so I came out and asked, "Ms. Cherry, why are they late? Aren't they coming to get me?"

She laughed out loud and shook her head. "Joyce, don't you start. The people on the outside are worrying us to death. The press is calling here every five minutes to ask if you've left yet. Stop fretting. They'll be here soon and you'll be on your way."

There were a few more goodbyes to get through. Logan and I walked through the administration building, the dining hall, and finally the E&R building, saying good-bye to all the teachers and staff. Finally I looked at Logan and said, "I think I need to go back to the dorm."

Quickly she guided me back to my empty cubicle where the two of us were able to spend some quiet time together. Sitting on my bed, she looked at me with tears in her eyes and said ever so softly, "Sis, I want you to go, I really do. But I already feel an emptiness inside."

There was nothing else to say. You go through life and have lots of acquaintances and lots of people you call friends, but it is rare to meet that one solitary person you can truly look at who becomes a part of you, an extension of yourself. That's what Logan and I were to each other.

Finally, a guard announced, "Joyce, the sergeant is coming."

Not one, but two sergeants escorted me down. One walked in front of me and one behind, both with walkie-talkies. I started worrying again. What was going on? Usually, when it was time for an inmate to depart, she was simply told to report to the Count Office. Later I found out that my method of departure was actually prison policy. With all the media hanging around, they decided to do it right for once.

As we passed the Count Office, Lieutenant Moore, an officer I had come to respect, stepped out of his office, threw his arms around me, and said, "Joyce, I don't ever want to see you in here again."

"You won't see me, lieutenant, unless it's on this case."

He smiled down at me. "You won't be back on this case, Joyce." As far as I know, it was the first time that the very proper and rigid Lieutenant Moore had ever hugged an inmate.

I was marched to the front gate where they allowed me to change into civilian clothes. Warden Craig was there, and when I got to the car she said, "Joyce, I'm so glad to get rid of you. If I had to talk to one more reporter, I think I would have gone stark raving mad." Then she wished me good luck and handed me over to the sheriff's deputies.

They opened the car door and handcuffed me. While I looked back at what had been my home for so many years, all that struck me was how truly drab the place was. I took a deep breath, waved goodbye to those watching, and slipped into the back seat.

The trip back was uneventful except for one ironic detail.

Two other inmates rode with me. A white girl sat in the middle and on her other side was a young black girl. I looked at the black girl for a while and finally figured out why she looked so familiar. She had pulled chain with me when I returned from my last hearing. At that time, she kept telling the deputies, "You've got the wrong person. I'm not supposed to be going to T.D.C. I haven't even been to trial yet."

Not until they got her to the Gatesville Unit was it discovered that she was right. The county jail had made a mistake and sent her down to prison before she had even had a trial.

When we arrived at the Lew Starrett Jail, the media surrounded the car. The two inmates with me got out on the other side and then I stepped out. Camera flashes began to go off and my head was bouncing from one person to another as everyone began shouting questions at once. I felt like I was going around in circles, circles, circles and finally said, "I would really like to stand here and answer your questions, but I have a family waiting in there to see me. I'm going to have to go."

We went inside to begin the usual long intake process but an officer stopped me. "You two ladies go in there. Joyce, you wait right here."

Then he took the handcuffs off me. I felt like running right that minute before something could happen to spoil my happiness. But I stood rock still while he said, "You've got a family out there waiting on you and what we're going to do is step around the corner here into the judge's chambers. He's going to come in, sign some papers, and within a couple of minutes you can walk out that door."

As simple as that.

As the officer promised, the signing of the papers took only a few minutes. When he had signed everything, the judge asked, "Joyce, do you remember me?"

I did indeed. It was the same judge who presided over my preliminary hearing when I was first arrested in 1980. I took a deep breath, looked around the room, and smiled. There was Kerry, and Jack, and Jim, and way in the back, standing in a corner, was Allen Weisman from *60 Minutes*. He was not there to cover the story or anything like that. Allen had flown in from New York, on his own time, his own money, just to be there when I got out. He believed in me so much that he simply wanted to be on hand when I was released.

Then someone opened the door for me and at 3:00 on the afternoon of November 3, 1989, I stepped outside—no handcuffs, no escort, no prison uniform.

Standing in front were Koquice and Brittainy. I grabbed them, then grabbed MaDear, and we hugged each other, crying, while the rest of my family and friends gathered around. It was the moment I had prayed for, waited for, lived for.

What a day! What a night! Yes, there was a party in the entertainment room of Mama's apartment complex. Hundreds, literally hundreds of people dropped by. I hugged and kissed more people that night than I had hugged and kissed in a lifetime. Relatives who had stood by me; friends I had not seen since being sent away; people I didn't even know who simply dropped by to wish me well. The "Victory Celebration" lasted well into the night.

By 4:00 a.m., I was absolutely exhausted. All four of us—MaDear, Koquice, Brittainy and I—crawled into Mama's big double bed. As I snuggled up close to MaDear, holding my granddaughter in my arms, it was then I knew I had come home.

I wasn't truly free, however. District Attorney John Vance announced that he fully intended to seek a retrial sometime in the spring (the former prosecutor in my case, Norman Kinne, had mysteriously faded out of the trial picture). This surprised many who thought the case would never come to trial due to the discrediting of Martha Jean Bruce. But despite all the evidence Kerry, Jim and Richard and the *60 Minutes* people had brought out, despite the fact that the very integrity of the D.A.'s office was under serious scrutiny, and despite rumors about the impact the case might have on the upcoming primary election, the district attorney claimed he wanted a retrial. This time, I wanted it too.

But that would come in the spring. Right now, there were lots of holidays to spend with my family and loved ones—Thanksgiving, Christmas, New Year's, birthdays, anniversaries—in fact, every day for the next few months was a holiday for me. Just waking up in the morning when I wanted to was a holiday. Lying in a tub of hot, bubbly water for as long as I wanted. Going into the bathroom and being able to close the door.

I spent day after day being domestic, and I loved every minute of it. Cooking for my family, baby-sitting my granddaughter and nieces and nephews, and cleaning house for Mary and MaDear.

Even the old familiar family squabbles were enjoyable.

Thanksgiving Eve, MaDear and I were in the kitchen from midnight until six, preparing the meal for the multitudes who would be on hand to celebrate with us. I was cooking and Mama was walking behind me like a shadow, checking everything I did. "No, no, let me see. No, don't put no more salt in there. Here, put some of this in there. You have the heat up too high on that. Stir that. Put a lid on that pot."

"MaDear," I finally said, "if I cook Christmas dinner I can promise you that you are not going to be anywhere near this kitchen. You're driving me crazy!"

Right after New Year's, I sat down with Kerry, Jack, and a few friends, and a trial strategy was developed. The district attorney was being coy about naming a date, but we had to assume that it would fall, as he had indicated, sometime in the spring. With Kerry and Jack concentrating on my legal defense, I addressed the problem of raising money and public support. With the help of my good friend Eva Miles, I began a campaign of personal fundraising appearances, complete with "Justice For Joyce" tee shirts and bumper stickers.

Jay began handling the requests from churches and schools who wanted me to make speeches to their children about prison life and what to expect if they didn't "Say No To Drugs."

I was touched by the reception I received at all these events. Everyone was sympathetic to my case and angered to learn that something like this could happen within the legal system. More importantly, many vowed to contact the district attorney's office and make their feelings known.

I also appeared on local television and radio talk shows, discussing prison life and answering questions called in by viewers and listeners. Inevitably, during the question and answer session I would be asked, "How can we help you?"

Whenever that question arose, I urged the callers to make their views known to the D.A.

Whatever could be done, I did it in order to get my story out to the public. And the public responded. Several reporters told Kerry they were hearing rumors to the effect that the district attorney was planning to make an announcement soon regarding my case. Finally, during the last week of January, Kerry called to inform me that an announcement would be made on February 15. Two weeks later, on February 12, Kerry called me again and advised me that the announcement had been pushed up to February 14th, and would be held in Judge Ron Chapman's Court at 10:00 a.m.

"We don't know what the meeting is for, but we have to assume that they will announce whether they are going to retry you or dismiss the charges."

"What will all that mean?" I asked.

"It means that if they announce they will retry you, Jack and I will get ready to do battle. If they drop the charges, you can walk out and not have this hanging over your head any more."

I asked him what the odds were.

"It could go either way." Kerry answered. "We'll just have to wait and see." Then he told me to call Jay and have him drive me to the court on the 14. He didn't want a large crowd present at the hearing. Then, he said, "Keep your fingers crossed and say a prayer or two, Joyce."

He didn't need to tell me that. I was praying as hard as I could.

I had contradictory feelings. I wanted it to all be over, but I also wanted to clear my name. The only way to do that was to go back to trial. I tried to sit back and take it as it came.

On Valentine's Day, 1990, Jay picked me up at Mary's at 9:00 a.m. It was a rainy, windy, overcast day. Adding to the gloom, traffic was backed up on the interstate and as we crept along, I was sure we would be late. I saw Kerry and Jack frantic with worry, the district attorney suggesting that the hearing wasn't important enough for me to be on time, and Judge Chapman getting impatient and leaving.

But we made it with three minutes to spare. Jay and I rushed up to the sixth floor and the first person we saw was Steve Blow. "They've postponed the hearing until tomorrow."

Jay and I looked at each other. "Are you sure?" he asked Steve.

"That's what one of the television reporters told me."

"Well, let's check it out," Jay said and we walked into the clerk's office.

The lady behind the desk verified that the hearing had been postponed until the following day, but a stocky black man standing nearby spoke up. "That's not true. The hearing has been postponed for an hour. We're scheduled for 11:00 instead of 10:00."

"How do you know?" Jay asked him.

"Because I'm Robert West, the assistant district attorney."

The man with the answer to my future. He looked straight past me.

We went back outside, chatted with friends and reporters, and then Kerry and Jack arrived. "Are you ready, kid?" Kerry wanted to know.

Part of me wanted to run out of the building and never come back. Part of me was ready to give the Dallas D.A. the fight of its life. I shrugged my shoulders. Whatever went down, I could handle.

Kerry put his arm around my shoulder and we walked into the court room. I sat down at the table, next to Jack and Kerry. The room was quiet. Finally Judge Chapman entered the chambers. We all rose, and as he sat down, he began talking.

"Did someone change the time on the docket?"

Kerry nodded.

"The judge is always the last to know." He studied some papers for a moment and looked up at the district attorney. "You have an announcement to make, Mr. West?"

"Yes, your Honor." And he began to talk. It was a very brief announcement. So brief that I barely realized he had started speaking before he sat down again.

Kerry put his hand on my shoulder. "That's it."

Now I was really confused. "That's all there is to it?"

"It's over, Joyce. You can go home. The district attorney has dropped the charges. You've won." He and Jack beamed with joy and gave me a minute to take it all in.

Judge Chapman left the courtroom. The district attorney put his papers back into his briefcase. And I just sat there, clutching my purse in my lap. It wasn't a pardon. It wasn't a parole. It wasn't even an apology. But at last, after nine years, five months and twenty-four days, my nightmare was over.